WHAT PEOPLE

PAGAN PORTALS:

Fairy Witchcraft is a very well researched study on Fairy beliefs, folklore and Morgan's personal experience with these entities. I found this book to be full of great and useful information as I continue my studies in the craft.
Peter Lucibelli, singer/songwriter on "Waiting For You"

Morgan Daimler takes you on a journey into the fascinating world of faery witchcraft, lovely book on a wonderful subject.
Rachel Patterson, author of *Pagan Portals Kitchen Witchcraft & Grimoire of a Kitchen Witch*

This much-needed book on the art and practice of Fairy Witchcraft is both informative and enjoyable. Morgan Daimler presents the traditional lore and workings of the fairy world in a way that is practical to explore and deep in its understanding.
David Salisbury, author of *The Deep Heart of Witchcraft*

A heartfelt guide to drawing on the power and magic of the Sidhe. Fairy Witchcraft is a must read for anyone interested in connecting and working with the Fairy realm.
Stephanie Woodfield, author of *Celtic Lore and Spellcraft of the Dark Goddess: Invoking the Morrigan*

Pagan Portals
Fairy Witchcraft

Pagan Portals
Fairy Witchcraft

Morgan Daimler

MOON
BOOKS

Winchester, UK
Washington, USA

First published by Moon Books, 2014
Moon Books is an imprint of John Hunt Publishing Ltd., Laurel House, Station Approach,
Alresford, Hants, SO24 9JH, UK
office1@jhpbooks.net
www.johnhuntpublishing.com
www.moon-books.net

For distributor details and how to order please visit the 'Ordering' section on our website.

Text copyright: Morgan Daimler 2013

ISBN: 978 1 78279 343 4

A CIP catalogue record for this book is available from the British Library.

Design: Lee Nash

Printed and bound by CPI Group (UK) Ltd, Croydon, CR0 4YY

We operate a distinctive and ethical publishing philosophy in all
areas of our business, from our global network of authors to
production and worldwide distribution.

CONTENTS

Call of the Fairy Witch

The Fair Folk are with us still
In lonely wood and hollow hill
Reaching out to those who hear
Crossing boundaries to be near
Faery music on the wind
calls us back to who we've been
So the Witch who hears the call
takes a path unlike them all...

Introduction

There seems to be an endless fascination with the world of Faery and its inhabitants. Fairies appear in myths and folklore around the world and have done for as long we have evidence of people telling stories. The term 'fairy' is a general word that can describe any being that is not clearly categorized as an angel or demon, and usually not a human ghost although there is some crossover between the dead and fairies. There are different theories about the physicality of fairies, with some people believing they are entirely incorporeal while others see them as having physical bodies. I tend to believe both are true; fairies are a diverse lot and can appear in many shapes and guises. In stories fairies appear as both helpers and dangers, sometimes both; because fairies operate on a totally different system of etiquette they can be easily offended through our ignorance. Traditionally, people who dealt with fairies often avoided saying the word fairy or even using the specific names for types of fairies, instead using euphemisms like 'Fair Folk', 'Good Neighbors', or 'Gentry'. This was done to avoid offending them and to keep from drawing any negative attention. Fairies can bless people with amazing good luck, health, the return of lost items, and even unexpected wealth, but they can also cause invisible injuries, madness, and otherwise torment people. The Celtic Fairy Faith grew out of the attempts by people in Celtic countries to live in harmony with the fairies and to create a system of protections and counter-magics for dealing with the dangerous ones.

As the modern Witchcraft movement has grown and diversified there has been a natural gravitation by some people towards the old Fairy Faith and its beliefs and practices. There is a lot of wisdom in the Fairy Faith and a great deal of tradition. Over the past few decades there have been several attempts to blend fairy beliefs with modern Witchcraft with varied results.

Usually, the systems that are created, heavily favor more New Age views or emphasize a largely eclectic Wiccan structure with a few friendly-fairy flourishes. If you are like me and take a more old-fashioned view, then the existing books on traditions that combine fairy belief and Witchcraft just don't work for you. This book is my attempt at offering seekers something different, something closer to the old Fairy Faith but with modern neopagan aspects..

I need to say several things up front. My view of fairies is strictly traditional – what you'll find in the old stories and myths – and so encompasses both the good and the bad; this can be at odds with the more popular neo-pagan views. My views are based on both what I have read and my own experiences, some of which I will share here. I have chosen to call the beliefs and practices I am writing about here Fairy Witchcraft to make it easier to identify for people seeking it, but I don't actually call my Witchcraft anything particular – it's just what I do and I don't need a special name for it. What I'm presenting here is the essence of my personal practice of Witchcraft and Fairy Faith, developed over the past 22 years, offered as a guidebook for those who want to follow the same approach.

I have seen and interacted with fairies since I was a small child. When I was very little I used to build houses for them out of small stones and branches, making them as detailed as possible. I would write notes to the fairies and leave them out on windowsills or walk out into the woods around my house at twilight and talk into the wind. I left little offerings – crystals, bits of food and drink, jewelry – and would find fairy gifts in return. Luckily my family treated this with amused tolerance and even subtly nurtured my beliefs with family stories and history. When I first encountered eclectic Witchcraft it merged seamlessly with my existing beliefs about the Otherworld and its inhabitants. As I began reading books by Yeats, Evans Wentz, Gregory and Lady Wilde I found that the stories they told matched my own experiences perfectly. I learned to use my own experiences and these authors as a measuring stick for new material; that which was too at odds with it was discarded. Over the years this slowly formed the Fairy Witchcraft I follow today.

Everything that follows should be taken and understood as my own opinions and beliefs on these subjects; where possible I will of course provide references to source material. Effectively I am trying to offer a resource for people who want to follow a Fairy Witchcraft but are unable to find any good material and don't want to take the time to create a practice from scratch. I have been honoring the fairies almost all my life and have been a Witch since 1991 – this then is the heart of my own practice of Witchcraft. I've never talked much publicly about it before, preferring to stick to discussing my Druidism or the Fairy Faith more generally, but I feel that now is the time to be more open. Maybe I can help other seekers find ways to connect to a path that is by its very nature obscure and hard to find.

Fairy Witchcraft FAQs

What is Fairy/Faery/Fairie Witchcraft?

The short answer is that it's a term used to describe any type of Witchcraft that includes or focuses on the fairies.

The long answer is that there are many different types and varieties of Fairy Witchcraft to be found, often reflections of a single individual's practices and opinions. Almost all of these are modern adaptations or creations; arguably only practices like British cunningcraft or the Irish fairy doctors could be seen as a continuation of older Fairy Witchcraft. Most modern types, including what you will find here, are attempts to synthesize the old fairy beliefs with neo-pagan Witchcraft. Some types will use a very narrow view of fairies while others, mine included, take the wider view.

What are Fairies?

Fairy is a catch-all term for any Otherworldly being, excluding angels and demons, and usually excluding human ghosts although humans can sometimes be among the ranks of Faery. Fairies are called different things among different cultures, but I will use the term fairy here for simplicity's sake. Fairies existed before people and as beings are usually more powerful than people, which is why it is wise to keep on their good side. I personally reject the idea of fairies as spirit guides, in the general sense, or benevolent beings, and see them instead as encompassing a wide range of beings with a wide range of motives, inclinations, and reactions to humans. Faeries can include everything from tiny garden spirits to human-appearing demi-Gods. They may be purely energy beings or they can be flesh and blood. They can be kindly inclined towards us or see us as a tasty snack. They may live in the wild or in our homes. Basically they are as diverse a group as you can imagine. Fairies can use their magic to influence us for good or ill, by changing our luck, our health, or using glamor to mislead us.

What is Witchcraft?

Generally, Witchcraft is a collection of practices designed to use folk magic to influence life. Witchcraft can also be practiced as a religion in its own right when different neo-pagan beliefs are incorporated in to it.

What is Fairy Witchcraft?

The Fairy Witchcraft you will find here is a way to bring the old Fairy Faith ways and beliefs forward into a modern neo-pagan context. The Fairy Faith is a belief system that transcends religion and so can be followed within any religion. However, it may be uniquely suited to combining with paganism. When a neo-pagan Witch chooses to follow the Fairy Faith and blend the two together the result is a new system, which I am calling Fairy

Witchcraft, which uses elements of the beliefs and practices of both to create a whole. It is a way not just to honor the fairies, but also to connect to them and to the Otherworld on a deeper level.

What Makes Fairy Witchcraft Different from Other Types of Neo-Pagan Witchcraft?

In many ways it is the same; however, some of the basic tools used are different, such as the Fairy Stone, and it has a much stronger emphasis on practices associated with British Hedge Witchcraft or cunningcraft, such as crossing the hedge (spiritual journey work), partnering with spirits (in this case fairies), healing, making offerings, and connecting to the Otherworld in general. Circle casting is sometimes used, but the purpose is slightly different, and so is the ritual structure.

What are the Holy Days of Fairy Witchcraft?

Fairy Witchcraft follows the same eight holidays as mainstream neo-pagan Witchcraft and also celebrates the full and dark moons each month, but the focus of each holiday is slightly different. While the Gods are honored at each holiday, each one also has significance within the Fairy Faith, which is acknowledged and the emphasis in the lunar celebrations is more on connecting to and honoring the Otherworld.

Group versus Solitary?

It is possible to practice Fairy Witchcraft in a small group, but I think it works best as a solitary effort. Each person's connection to Faery will be unique and experiential, making group work very challenging unless the group is very tight-knit or experienced together.

Can Anyone Follow this Path?

Yes and no. Anyone can choose to follow the path of Fairy Witchcraft, but whether or not the fairies will respond is impossible to say. Some people spend a lifetime trying to nurture a relationship with the fairies and never get any response while others would just as soon not have anything to do with them and yet are always surrounded by spirits. There are two parts to being a Witch on a fairy path: one is to include honoring them in your practice but the other is to actively interact with them in your magics. The first is possible even without fairy attentions but the second can never be achieved without a reciprocal relationship.

Do We Worship the Fairies?

No. We worship the old Gods, but we do not worship the fairies. We honor and respect them and make offerings to them, because they have the ability to help or harm us. The fairies can be our allies and friends if we are able to earn those relationships in our practice.

Chapter 1

Getting Started

The first step along the path of practicing Fairy Witchcraft is to find and read as much folklore about fairies as possible. I recommend books by William Butler Yeats, Lady Gregory, Eddie Lenihan, Katherine Briggs, and Brian Froud. Fairies have a different culture and different expectations of behavior than humans and it is important to understand this before trying to create any kind of relationship with them. This understanding is essential for the practice of Fairy Witchcraft. Entire books have been written just on the how-to of interacting with fairies and it is beyond the scope of this work to cover every aspect of it, but here are some key points:

- Faeries are found in every culture of the world, as far as I am aware. In the Irish they might be called daoine sidhe, the people of the fairy hills, in the Norse they could be called the Alfar or more generally landvaettir. To the Cherokee they are the Yunwi Tsundsi, the Little People. For simplicity in this book we call them all fairies. Usually euphemisms are used for them which are intended to invoke their pleasant or good aspects and these include: Good Neighbors, People of Peace, The Other Crowd, Mother's Blessing, the Wee Folk, the Little People, the Gentry, Fair Folk , and the Shining Ones.
- Faeries prefer people who are kind, generous, and happy. Nurturing these qualities tends to draw fairies to you. Conversely being cruel and stingy often repulses fairies.
- Never say thank you to fairies. Although you should always repay a gift with a gift and show proper gratitude; saying thank you is offensive to fairy folk. There are

7

different theories as to why this is, some people believe that saying thank you implies the fairies are your servants, others that it is dismissive, or that it creates a debt.

- Certain things are used as defenses against fairies; these include iron, black-handled knives, salt, rowan wrapped in red thread, St. John's wort, and broom. While these can be used to protect against fairies, you should keep areas clear of these items when you are trying to cultivate a relationship with them. The only exception is the black-handled knife, which can be used in Fairy Witchcraft for purposes of protection magic and spells, if the blade is not made of iron.

- Fairies can be found anywhere, from wild natural places to the city, from the seaside to your house. They are liminal beings who live in both our world and the Otherworld and it is in their natures to cross boundaries.

- Fairies can be as tiny as ants or may be giants. They can appear as animals or be human seeming, beautiful or hideously ugly. Some fairies may exist only as energetic beings while others have solid physical bodies; some may be both. A small number of fairies may look like the Victorian idea of fairies, small and child-like with wings, but most are wingless and can otherwise appear young or old. In many stories of fairies from Ireland they are described as looking much like people but clearly not being humans.

- Fairies are masters of a type of magic called glamor which uses illusion to make a person perceive one thing as being another, so that a pile of leaves might seem to be a stack of gold or a dreary cave may seem to be a grand castle chamber. This means that when dealing with fairies nothing is ever exactly what it seems to be.

- One should never eat or drink the food of Faery, lest you be trapped there forever.

- Time in Faery runs differently than time in the mortal world. In folklore, people taken into Fairyland may believe they have been gone for a year when only a single night has passed or think that one night has gone by when they have actually been gone for seven years.
- Fairies can influence people's lives by affecting their health or luck, but they can also steal items and lead people astray, give gifts, and teach people magic.
- Never lie to a fairy, never make a promise you can't keep and don't break your word.
- Those with second sight or spirit sight can see fairies, as well as ghosts and other spirits, and may be able to see through fairy glamor. People without this ability can enhance it by carrying a four-leaf clover or wearing lapis lazuli. Otherwise fairies may choose to be visible or invisible to humans.
- Fairies are easily offended and insulted so it is important to always be polite and respectful. Generally one should not speak of personal experiences with the fairies or gifts received from them, although there are some exceptions to this.
- Dealing with fairies is always a tricky business and while it can be very enriching it can also have its dangers. If you have children it would be wise to place a bit of iron beneath their mattresses or hang a bit of broom or some rowan and red thread over their beds. Horseshoes can be hung over the doorways of rooms that you do not want fairies in.
- Green is a fairy color and is often associated with them.
- Fairies can be found in liminal places, but also in certain locations that can include lone hills, solitary trees, especially hawthorn trees, abandoned houses, in fairy rings, and along special paths called fairy roads.

Once you have a thorough grounding in fairy lore the next step is to start learning trance and spiritual journey practices; I recommend Diana Paxson's book *Trance-Portation*. This is important because one aspect of the practice of Fairy Witchcraft is what Traditional Witches call crossing the hedge, or traveling to the Otherworlds. This is something that takes years of practice and is a developed skill.

It's important for followers of this path to study the history of Celtic Witchcraft as well as fairy folklore. Although the basic structure of Fairy Witchcraft is based on blending the Fairy Faith and neo-pagan Witchcraft, the core idea behind it is the long-standing association between Witches and fairies in Celtic countries. Both Witches and fairies in Irish folklore have many things in common, both being given some of the same attributes and both being feared for their ability to curse and bewitch cattle or to heal and bless. The relationship between Witches and fairies is a longstanding one, with some well-known Witches, like Biddy Early, being said to have learned from the fairies and to use a fairy gift in their work.

It's important to study the history of both fairies and Witches to see and understand how the two were thought to overlap because that helps us to see the ways that our practice can be structured. For example, Irish Witches were well known to be able to take the shapes of both hares and weasels. There are several stories of farmers or hunters who are out in the early morning and spot a hare in among the cows, shoot it, and find later that a well-known neighbor has been injured, having been the Witch shape-changed (O hOgain, 1995; Wilde, 1991). It is perhaps because of this association that it is thought to be bad luck for a hare to cross your path (Wilde, 1991). Similarly, Witches could take the form of a weasel and it was thought to be bad luck to cross paths with any weasel in the morning, although it was equally bad luck to kill it and risk its spirit seeking revenge (Wilde, 1991). It should be kept in mind though, that as with so many things in Irish folklore, it could always be the fairies; indeed fairies were known to take the form of hares as well, particularly white ones (O hOgain, 1995). Both Witches and fairies were thought to shapeshift, so shapeshifting in spirit would be a skill developed by followers of Fairy Witchcraft.

Through The Veil – Pixy-led

Many years ago I had a loose assortment of friends who were all different types of pagans. One full moon we decided to get together and have a ritual and one woman mentioned a spot out in the woods that she had used many times. We all met up in early afternoon and then drove out to the suburban home where her parents lived, before hiking back into the woods about a mile or so.

The ritual location was lovely and we had a casual ceremony followed by a long, pleasant conversation that lasted into the early evening. Finally, it was full dark, and even with the full moon above us the forest was closing in so we packed up and started back. After walking for about five minutes we could clearly see the lights from the houses shining through the trees ahead of us. But after ten more minutes the lights were no closer. We climbed over rocks and around trees, through thorns and fallen branches, yet never seemed able to move forward. One other friend and I began to suspect fairy enchantment, as the rest of the group fought to push forward.

Finally, after perhaps another 15 minutes of walking, my friend and I acknowledged that we were being pixy-led; we began to laugh and compliment the fairies on such a fine joke. The energy broke with an almost physical snap and within a few minutes we emerged in a backyard a few houses down from where we'd first gone into the woods.

Chapter 2

Beliefs

There are several basic beliefs of Fairy Witchcraft. The first, of course is belief in fairies, which is obviously an essential component. However one chooses to define what fairies are, one must believe they exist in order to follow this spirituality. From a traditional standpoint defining 'fairy' is difficult as the word is used to encompass a wide range of spirits and in Fairy Witchcraft the entire range of these spirits may be dealt with, from the malicious to the benign.

Every culture has its own approach to fairies and different beliefs associated with them; Fairy Witchcraft mainly uses the beliefs and practices of the Celtic Fairy Faith, but also incorporates other fairy beliefs. An individual following this path would be encouraged to study folklore of any culture and see how it could be synthesized with the existing beliefs.

Generally speaking we see fairies as independent, intelligent beings of varying levels of Power. Fairies are often divided up into groupings of good and bad faeries, which are called the Seelie and Unseelie courts by some, depending on whether they are helpful or harmful to us. It is rarely as simple as that though, with individual fairies switching from one group to another depending on mood and interaction with us; for example a Brownie is a helpful house spirit but when offended becomes a dangerous Boggart. Some fairies are always dangerous or always kind, but the majority of fairies are somewhere in the middle and may be either depending on how we treat them. A fairy normally considered 'bad' may choose to help an individual and a fairy usually seen as 'good' might harm a person, so the words good and bad are used rather loosely and fluidly. Within Fairy Witchcraft we seek to nurture relationships with certain individual fairy beings that support our magical practices.

Fairies can be found in every culture under different names. Wherever you live there will be fairies around you and although the different cultures may interpret them slightly differently there is a common thread. Although it is important to study folklore, including local myths and stories, what really matters is less what you choose to call each individual Being and more about learning to relate to them and interact with them safely and respectfully.

As a general rule we do not consider elemental beings to be fairies, or vice versa, but rather see elementals as a separate class of beings. Whereas fairies by nature are liminal creatures that cross boundaries, elementals are defined by the single element they embody. The idea of elementals, elemental rulers, and directional correspondences is rooted in alchemy and is largely foreign to the traditional Fairy Faith. This is one of the ways that we strongly differ from many other modern Witchcraft traditions.

We also believe in ghosts, or human spirits that are earthbound. Some ghosts attach themselves to specific human families or homes while others may wander or stay near certain places. In some cases the line between the dead and the fairies can be a blurry one and it is possible for a person thought to be dead to appear among the fairy ranks; it may be that the person was actually taken by the fairies. Fairies and the dead also appear together in some accounts of the Wild Hunt.

We believe that there are many worlds beyond our own existence. One of these is the Otherworld of the fairies, although the Otherworld itself is likely more than one place. The Otherworld exists as a place that is connected to, but separated from, our reality and can be reached through natural openings as well as created gateways. There are also different worlds as well, including the Spirit world and realm of the Gods.

Another key belief of Fairy Witchcraft is animism, or the belief that all things have a spirit, and this goes along with the belief in fairies. Often the animistic spirit of a place or thing may be called a fairy, as it would fit into that broad category. Working with these spirits of place and the spirits of plants and trees is animistic in nature but we relate to them as fairy beings.

Animism is a cornerstone of Fairy Witchcraft so it deserves a more in-depth explanation. In effect, animism is the belief that animals (including people), plants, natural objects and phenomena, and sometimes man-made objects have a spirit. An animistic world view can be found in all cultures at varying points and psychologist Jean Paiget theorized that animism is the natural state of belief in children.

Unlike pantheism, which sees all existence as having a unified spirit, animism sees each spirit as unique; my soul is not the same soul as yours, nor is one oak the same spirit as another oak, although we do also believe in larger unifying spirits as well. So this oak has a unique spirit as does that oak but there is also a spirit of Oak that is universal to all oaks, for example. Another thing that makes animism different from some other viewpoints is that to an animist all spirits are generally equal in significance (not, however, in Power) so that a human spirit is no more or less important in the universe than a maple, or a squirrel, or a river. Animism does not see humans as superior or inherently more worthy than anything else. This does not mean that to an individual human, or group of humans, their lives mean less, but rather that they do not interact with the world with the idea that they are privileged; the spirits around them must be treated with respect in order for the humans themselves to succeed.

When I say I am an animist I mean that I perceive the world as being populated by spirits, in the sense described above. Material existence cannot be separated from spirit, because spirit is an integral part of all things and is manifest in the individual spirits that inhabit the world. My cats have spirits, just as I and my family do. The oaks, maples, aspen, and cedars in my yard have souls, as does the swamp behind my house. As a modern animist I believe my car also has a spirit and that any piece of man-made technology can eventually develop a spirit. Animism also shapes my belief that spirits are eternal, and so just because something has died doesn't mean its spirit is destroyed and this goes along with the belief in reincarnation which I jokingly refer to as 'spirit recycling'.

It is important to live in right relation with the spirits we share the world with, just as much as we should live in right relation with our human neighbors and co-workers (and for much the same reason). This can be done by showing respect and gratitude, taking only what we need, and using everything we take. It also means seeing the world around us as full of living spirits that are just as important as we are. I have a certain horror at the wanton, purposeless, destruction and death that is so common in a world that will clear an area of land to sell and then let it all sit and rot waiting for a non-existent buyer, or pollute and poison an area for expediency.

Both our view of fairies and this animism avoid the dichotomous thinking that says a thing is either totally good or bad, or the view that all is good; it teaches us that there are good spirits and bad spirits, yes, but also that most spirits are simply spirits that will respond based on how they are treated. And most importantly it disabuses us of the idea that we are privileged or special; whether we like it or not we are as valuable as everything else in the grand scheme of life and when working with fairies we are often not only not the most powerful beings but also not at the top of the food chain, either.

We believe in reincarnation, that is that the soul is eternal and when the body dies the soul is reborn into a new body. Between lives the soul may remain earthbound as a ghost, may live in the Otherworld, may protect the family line, or may rest in the spirit world. Human and animal souls reincarnate and it is possible for the soul to take different forms. As Fairy Witches, although we believe in reincarnation we also honor the spirits of our ancestors, believing that those who cared about us in life still watch over us in death. We honor our ancestors by telling the stories of their lives and by lighting candles for them.

The ancestors are regularly honored in Fairy Witchcraft, although exactly how this is done is up to the Witch. Some people may choose to keep a token, such as a (replica) skull, on their altar to represent their ancestors while others may choose to have a separate small altar for the ancestors which may contain pictures and tokens of people who have passed.

Fairy Witchcraft is a polytheistic paganism which embraces a belief in many Gods. Generally speaking, someone following this path would either be drawn to or seek out deities that are historically associated with the fairies. This is simple in the Irish pantheon, as the Irish Gods, the Tuatha de Danann, were said to have gone into the fairy hills and become the aos sidhe, or fairy people. Researching almost any Irish deity will reveal connections to Faery. In other cultures Gods can also be found with similar associations to the Otherworld and its inhabitants, including deities like Odin in the Norse pantheon and Hecate in the Greek and Roman pantheons.

Another option for the Fairy Witch is to follow the primal unnamed Gods.

We each connect to these older natural forces in our own ways. They are deeply personal, representing an intimate connection to the liminal place between the living green world and the timeless Otherworld. I call them by titles: the Lady of the Greenwood, the Lord of the Wildwood, the Hunter, the Queen of the Wind. Not creative titles, but descriptive ones. There is something utterly foreign and achingly familiar about them that I cannot put into words. They are primal. They are wild. They are experiential. I have no frame of reference for them outside my own experience, no myths, no folklore, no ancient texts to rely upon to understand them or how to honor them. Worshiping them is, perforce, an exercise in intuition and awareness; you must trust your own intuition and let yourself be aware – of their presence, of their preferences, of their patterns. You must let yourself abide in that primal place within, where these qualities, intuition and awareness are a language of their own.

These Gods are not tame or domesticated. They aren't Gods of computers, or the safety of the hearth fire. They live in the wild places of the world, in the heartbeat of animals that have never known a human hand, in the shadows of city buildings, in the endless mist and relentless tide. They dwell on the paths to Faery, in the music of the sidhe that haunts those who hear it, in bliss and in agony. They live in the perpetual twilight and the first rays of dawn, in the flood and the storm as well as the gentle rain. You can find them in the vast wilderness and in the twisting city streets. They are forces of change; they are unchanging. They are heartlessly brutal and unimaginably kind. They are grotesque; they are beautiful. They are all these things simultaneously and in harmony.

These are the liminal Gods. This is the heart of the pagan aspect of Fairy Witchcraft, the bridge between Fairy Faith practices and pagan religion, the forces that are greater Powers than the daoine sidhe and more immediate than the Gods from known pantheons. I do not have to seek them out; they are here. I speak to them beneath the moon and in the wind, amid the forest's song and the music of the rushing stream. I offer to them, pray to them, and hear their voices in synchronicity and dream.

Theirs is not an easy path to follow because it means letting go of the civilized expectations we hold with other Gods. It is a path through the trackless forests and the untouched wilds both within and without. It puts aside logic and rational thought and embraces instinct and emotion. And once you are on their path you cannot help but be changed by it. And once you are on their path there is no turning back.

The Lady of the Greenwood and the Lord of the Wildwood rule during the light half of the year, from Beltane until Samhain and are also honored on the full moon; the Hunter and the Queen of the Wind rule the dark half of the year from Samhain until Beltane and are honored on the dark moon. The Lady of the Greenwood is the soul of the living forest and the Lord of the Wildwood is the spirit of all that lives within it. The Hunter is the guardian of the animals of the winter wood and the Queen of the Wind is its spirit. Each exists within the other half of the year but they are strongest when they rule.

The Lady of the Greenwood is a Goddess of life, potential, growth, and healing. She nurtures and inspires, comforts and guides. She is the flower blooming in spring, the fruit ripening on the tree, the surge of new life. She is a Goddess of sexuality, fertility, and new beginnings.

The Lord of the Wildwood is a god of action and motion, of physical skill and health. He is the will to live and succeed, but also the nurturing masculine element. He is the hawk brooding on a nest, the stag rutting in the fall, and the crops waiting to be harvested. He is a God of adventure and exploration.

The Hunter is a god of contemplation, planning, and strategy. He is the ruthlessness of the hungry predator and the fierceness of the defending warrior. He is the guide to the Spirit world for those who have passed and the sharp blade that separates life from death. He is a God of wisdom, strength, and the dead.

The Queen of the Wind is a Goddess of introspection, renewal, and magic. She is the cold wind of winter that heralds snow and the warm wind of spring that melts the ice. She is the Queen of magic and divination, who sees without judgment, but she is also the inescapable breath of balance that creates harmony. She is the earth that holds the seeds waiting to grow next to the bones of the dead. She is a Goddess of enchantment, death, and rebirth.

Fairy Witchcraft works with three realms: sea, land, and sky; and five elements: earth, air, fire, water, and spirit. The realm of sea is related to islands in the west where the isles of the dead are said to be – along with many other fairy isles – and so sea is also associated with the ancestors. Ideally the ancestor altar is placed in the west, because of this association. Earth is our world and is associated with the Witch and with healing magic. Sky is associated with both the Gods and the slua sidhe, the dangerous fairies of the air. Representations of the three realms may be kept on the altar as symbols of our connection to them; these can be as simple as a seashell, stone, and feather. When the elements are invoked, for example when a circle is cast, all five are called in. Earth is in the north and represents strength, healing, and partnership; its color is black. Air is in the east and represents inspiration, intellect, and divination; its color is white. Fire is in the south and represents passion, ambition, and courage; its color is red. Water is in the west and represents compassion, ancestry, and emotion; its color is blue. Spirit is in the center and represents union, immanence, and connection; its color is purple. Additionally, each direction is associated with a season: spring is in the east, summer in the south, autumn in the west, and winter in the north (McNeil, 1956). Spirit represents the entire year.

Following the beliefs of the Fairy Faith all positive actions are done in a clockwise, or sunwise, direction. Moving sunwise is blessing and draws good luck. In contrast, moving against the sun is done for cursing or banishing. Ideally, sacred places should be circled three times before being entered, and in magic you turn or move sunwise for all positive and healing magics and against the sun for cursing and destructive magics. This includes not only walking but also stirring and other hand motions in magic; I stir sunwise when cooking food for my family and put a good word on the mixing to bless the food.

All of these beliefs woven together form the core of Fairy Witchcraft and it is from these beliefs that the practices naturally flow. In turn all the beliefs reinforce and support each other. Although the system stands alone perfectly well it is possible to further blend it into other forms of neo-paganism as well.

Through The Veil – Healing a Broken Place

In the area I live in there is a state park called Devil's Hopyard because of the mild seismic activity that occurs there. The area is widely recognized by local pagans as a sacred place and has many fairies, good and bad, inhabiting it. Last year during a prolonged dry spell a careless person tossed a cigarette and started a fire that burned over 100 acres of the forest. It took several days to be contained and longer for the full damage to be known.

A week after the fire I packed a small bag and headed out to the Hopyard. My normal parking spot was in an area that was unaffected; it sat in sun dappled splendor by the river that runs through the park. I hiked out beneath trees unfurling spring leaves, enjoying the welcoming energy of the land. I felt the fire long before I saw it, as the tang of burned wood in the air and a growing atmosphere of anger and resentment. My boots crunched through burned underbrush and ash, and my skin crawled. The spirits here were outraged. They were grieving. They were frightened. I found a slight depression at the base of a burned stone and knelt down; it was a struggle not to set the bag down on the scorched ground as I tried to open it. Glancing up I saw a figure, skin the color of bark, hair lank and hanging, glaring at me. I looked back down and gave up trying to keep the bag clean, dropping it onto the ground I pulled out a container of heavy cream, a bottle of fresh water, and an apple. Something rustled loudly off to my right. Using a stick I dug a shallow hole in the earth at the base of the rock.

I picked up the water, and said, 'May this place be healed.' Then I poured the water out over the stone.

Picking up the apple, I said, 'May this place be renewed.' Then I placed it next to the stone.

Finally, I picked up the cream and said, 'I am sorry for the pain people have caused here. I am sorry for the destruction. I am sorry. May this place be healed. May it be renewed. May there be friendship between us.' And I poured out the cream into the hole.

The wind sighed around me, lifting my hair. It felt as if the forest had let go of a breath it had been holding. Something moved again in the brush off to the right and then everything went still, but the tension was gone from the air.

I picked up my bag and turned to hike back to my car.

Chapter 3

Fairy Tools

The main tools of the Fairy Witch are the knife, cauldron, stone, wand, quaich, mortar and pestle and broom.

The first four, the knife, cauldron, stone, and wand, are based on the four Treasures of the Tuatha de Danann and each is symbolic of the mythic tool it is meant to represent.

> **305.** There were four cities in which they [the Tuatha de Danann] were acquiring knowledge and science and diabolism: these are their names, Failias, Goirias, Findias, Muirias. From Failias was brought the Lia Fail which is in Temair, and which used to utter a cry under every king that should take Ireland, From Goirias was brought the spear which Lug had: battle would never go against him who had it in hand. From Findias was brought the sword of Naudu: no man would escape from it; when it was drawn from its battle-scabbard, there was no resisting it. From Murias was brought the cauldron of The Dagda; no company would go from it unsatisfied.
>
> *Lebor Gabala Erenn* (MacAlister, 1941)

Alexei Kondrative in his book *Apple Branch* offers a good system based on using the treasures and four cardinal points; he uses the etymology of the names of the cities to associate them with the four classical elements and then to directions (Kondratiev, 1998). Although these differ from those used in Fairy Witchcraft, it can be useful to study his ideas and the thoughts behind them.

The treasures represent the values of sovereignty (stone), hospitality (cauldron), defense (wand), and offense (knife), respectively, all of which are important in Fairy Witchcraft.

The Stone

3. *From Falias was brought the Stone of Fal which was located in Tara. It used to cry out beneath every king that would take Ireland.* Gray, 1983

The Lia Fail is one of the most interesting of the treasures because it does not belong to any named Deity, but rather to the land of Ireland herself. Interestingly the Electronic Dictionary of the Irish Language (eDIL) gives multiple definitions to the Old Irish word Fal, and these include the stone at Tara, abundance, science and learning, a king, and a fence, hedge, or enclosure, and mentions that Fal was once used as a name for Ireland.

While in modern euphemism the Lia Fal is often called the Stone of Destiny, I tend to think of it as the stone of Ireland. It represents, literally and figuratively, the sovereignty of the island. In my practice I meditate on it as the expression of the will of the land and of the power of right leadership. As a personal symbol I see it as representing the importance of connecting to and living in right relationship with the land, and listening to her voice.

In Fairy Witchcraft the stone is placed on the altar as a symbol representing this same connection to the land. The stone itself should be found, as a gift from the fairies. This is in the tradition of the old curing stones in Celtic tradition; they might be green, black, white, or quartz, often river stones, and were usually special in some way. Believed to be given by the fairies or spirits, the stone has curative powers and is used in healing work as well as ritual. There are several well-known fairy stones such the one given to Coinneach Odhar, the Brahan Seer, who used a holed stone given him by the fairies for divination.

The Wand

4. *From Gorias was brought the spear which Lug had. No battle was ever sustained against it, or against the man who held it in his hand.*
Gray, 1983

The spear of Lugh is the next treasure mentioned, a fierce weapon that could overcome any battle. Lugh himself is the many-skilled God, destined to win the war against the Fomorians for the Tuatha de by slaying his grandfather Balor, and also a God who would be king of the Tuatha de. His spear is described as a weapon which no battle can be sustained against, a power that is extended to any who bear the spear. To me, I see the spear as having a more defensive energy to it, because of the way the translations word the description: 'No battle was ever sustained against it'. In this case the use of the word 'against' has a defensive feel to me (others may disagree of course). When I meditate on the spear I tend to see it as representing the value of a good defense, of standing your ground, and of persevering.

The spear correlates to the wand in Fairy Witchcraft. It's fairly well established that the wand was an important tool used by Celtic magic users and Druids in mythology. Wands were used not only as a sort of badge of office but also as a magical tool to direct and control energy, usually accompanied by a spoken charm. When we look at Irish mythology we see many instances of Druids using wands, as well as other magic users, such as Fionn mac Cumhail.

The story of Fionn includes the use of wands, generally made of hazel. It is a hazel wand that turns Fionn's wife into a deer, and in some translations it is a hazel wand that prospective members of the Fianna must use to defend themselves with when under-going trials before being accepted. One version of a story about Fionn has him using a hazel wand for divination (although most versions have him biting on his thumb). In some versions of the story of the Children of Lir, as well, a wand is used to curse the four children into the shape of swans and in The Wooing of Etain, the Druid Dalan uses three wands made of yew to divine the location of Etain.

A wand is also associated with the traditional celebration of Imbolc where a slat Brighid (wand of Brighid) is placed with the Brideog, in the hopes that the morning will reveal the marks of the wand in the fireplace ashes. The slat Brighid is described as a straight section of white wood, with bark peeled off, and is often made of birch, willow, or bramble (Carmicheal, 1900). In Scotland the quarter days were celebrated, in part, with the use of rowan wands, which were placed above the doors for protection and blessing (McNeill, 1956).

In Fairy Witchcraft wands are the main tool used for directing magical energy and casting spells; different woods are used for their unique properties. A healing spell, for example, may be cast with a willow wand while a protection spell may use an oak wand. A Fairy Witch may have many different wands, but should at least have wands of willow for healing, rowan for enchantment, and hazel for transformation.

Fairy Witchcraft encourages each Witch to study the plants and animals of the region the Witch lives in and to learn and use those materials, as wands made from local trees will have a stronger energy for the Witch. It is also important to have a connection to the tree the wood comes from when possible. However, we also rely on the folklore of the Irish Fairy Faith to create a correspondence system for the different trees. The trees used for magic and wand making were different in Ireland and in Britain; indeed the sacred trees themselves differed from the well-known British oak and its attendant mistletoe. Oak was known and mentioned as sacred in Ireland, but it is the hazel and rowan that were most well known (McNeill, 1956). It is believed that the ancient Irish revered hazel, rowan, elder, and hawthorn in particular, with yew and ash also mentioned in some sources (Estyn Evans, 1957; Wilde, 1991). Even into the last century hazel and rowan were viewed as protective and blessing in Irish folklore (O Suilleabhain, 1967).

The rowan was seen as a lucky wood and was considered to be the best protection against negative magic; it is also considered by some to provide the berries that are the food of the aos sidhe (McNeill, 1956). Rowans were often planted by the front door of the home to protect it and rowan wood was used to make sacred fires to cook the little cakes often featured in folk ceremonies (McNeill, 1956). Some also believe that rowan was the wood used by the Irish Druids to create sacred fires for their rituals (Estyn Evans, 1957). In modern practice, the rowan is sometimes associated with the Goddess Brighid. On Beltane, sprigs of rowan were hung above cradles, churns, and doorways to protect them from fairy influence (Wilde, 1991).

To the Irish, the hazel was both seen as useful in magic, as a wand, and also connected to wisdom as hazelnuts were believed to provide knowledge. We see this in the story of Fionn, who eats a salmon that has eaten the hazelnuts of the well of Segias and gains the wisdom of the world. Hazel nuts are associated with Samhain divinations and may have been used for the same purpose by the Druids (McNeill, 1956). Hazel is also associated with weather magic and with water, being seen by some as connected to storms and having a long history of use in water divining (McNeill, 1956).

It was believed that a hazel wand cut on Beltane had the greatest power, and that a person could use such a wand to trace a circle in the ground around themselves which would be a sure protection against fairies and evil spirits (Wilde, 1991). Besides protection, particularly from faeries, hazel was also associated with healing, especially from poison (Danaher, 1964). As we've noted, hazel wands appear in mythology used by Druids to transform and to divine.

The elder was also seen as significant. This tree was associated with protection and also with the faeries (McNeill, 1956). The elder seems to have a contradictory nature, being used for healing and making musical instruments like flutes, but also used in cursing; it is said that striking a living thing with an elder twig will cause illness or death (Danaher, 1964).

The apple has a long history in Irish lore, being associated with magic, healing, and long life. In myth the apple branch is used to gain entry to the Otherworld, and is strongly associated with the aos sidhe. As Evans Wentz says in the epic *Fairy Faith in Celtic Countries*, 'For us there are no episodes more important than those in the ancient epics concerning these apple-tree talismans, because in them we find a certain key which unlocks the secret of that world from which such talismans are brought, and proves it to be the same sort of a place as the Otherworld of the Greeks and Romans.' (Evans Wentz, 1911). Many modern Druids use an apple branch decked with bells to open the way to the Otherworld during ritual, and to invite in good spirits.

Both the blackthorn and hawthorn were dual natured, seen as both protective and also as fairy trees that could be dangerous (O Suilleabhain, 1967). The hawthorn has many associations with Beltane. It may have been significant in part because of its flowers and berries, with the white flowers representing the hope of spring and its red berries the fulfillment of the harvest (Estyn Evans, 1957). While hawthorns planted by people, or found in hedges, were not seen as special, the lone hawthorn was said to be a fairy tree and not to be disturbed or damaged (Estyn Evans, 1957). Hawthorn is considered one of the seven herbs of great power by Lady Wilde, along with elder tree bark, ivy, vervain, eyebright, groundsel, and foxglove (Wilde, 1991).

Finally, the yew also plays a role in the Irish approach to magical trees. As mentioned, we see a Druid using yew wands in The Wooing of Etain for the purpose of divination. The yew was renowned for its long life and was one of the trees about which it was thought that trimming would bring bad luck (Danaher, 1964). In modern folklore the yew is associated with death, but this is not likely to have been how the ancients saw it as the modern view is largely based on the fact that yews are often found growing in church graveyards.

Certain new world trees, such as the Maple, also play a role in Fairy Witchcraft. Maple represents peace, happiness, and friendship and can be used for any magic relating to those subjects. Additionally, products from the maple, including syrup and maple sugar can be used as offerings.

The Knife

5. From Findias was brought the sword of Nuadu. No one ever escaped from it once it was drawn from its deadly sheath, and no one could resist it.
Gray, 1983

Juxtaposing the spear is Nuada's sword, a clearly offensive weapon. Nuada was the king of the Tuatha de when they first came to Ireland and then again after his arm was healed. Unlike Lugh, who is described as many-skilled, Nuada seems to be a much more straightforward God of battle, married according to some sources, to battle Goddess Macha. Although some sources do connect him to healing he is clearly a deity of war and battle, leading the Gods in the epic wars. His sword is said to be inescapable once drawn, and unbeatable. Whereas the spear is described as a weapon against which no battle could be sustained, the sword is said to be something from which none escape. I tend to see the sword as representing a good offense, something that we all need to have at some point. Although ruthless, it is perhaps a lesson that any situation which calls for offensive action should be entered into with the intent of winning. The sword shows no mercy, and presents no weakness.

In my practice I will meditate on the sword as the attitude needed to achieve victory in any battle, and as the ability to fight for oneself and one's family.

In Fairy Witchcraft the knife represents the sword, and it is essential that it be of a metal that is not iron or steel. Many fairies abhor this metal and it is a common defense against them, so in our Witchcraft we do not use these metals. My own knife is of bronze. The knife in Fairy Witchcraft is a channel for personal power. The knife is used to direct energy when casting the circle and in healing work. In traditional healing practices illnesses are often treated as sentient beings and healing magic involves threatening the spirit of the illness in order to banish it. Because black-handled knives are traditionally used for protection, the Fairy Witchcraft knife should be black handled as it is also the main tool of protection for the Witch when dealing with dangerous spirits.

The Cauldron

6. *From Murias was brought the Dagda's cauldron. No company ever went away from it unsatisfied.*
Gray, 1983

Finally, we have the last treasure, the cauldron of the Dagda. It is not at all surprising to me that the Dagda, a God who himself is associated with great appetite and excess, would be the holder of such a cauldron. It is also worth noting that despite the modern neo-pagan association of the cauldron with feminine or Goddess energy, it is actually most often associated with Gods in Irish and more generally Celtic myth. The Dagda has the cauldron of plenty, the healing God Dian Cecht has a cauldron (sometimes called a spring) of healing, and even a Welsh story about Bran and Branwen that talks about an Irish king who has a cauldron that can revive the dead.

Additionally, we see the poem attributed to Amergin ,The Cauldron of Poesy, which describes three cauldrons born in every person. The cauldron itself is clearly a very powerful and widespread symbol in Celtic myth. The Dagda's cauldron is one of abundance that satisfies all who take from it, a fitting treasure for one who is sometimes called Eochaid Ollathair, the All-father. I tend to see it as a representation of the qualities of generosity and hospitality, as well as the ability of a leader or head-of-household to provide for those who look to them for support. When I meditate on the cauldron I see it in the light of a source of these things and try to relate that into my own life. I also often end up contemplating the wider symbolism of the cauldron in Irish myth as a provider of abundance and healing.

The cauldron in Fairy Witchcraft is a symbol of abundance, renewal, healing, and blessing. Unlike in many other forms of neo-pagan Witchcraft, the cauldron in Fairy Witchcraft is not associated with female or Goddess energy but is seen as a genderless source of creation; it is representative of the holy wells and of the ancient cauldrons of power. It is the central tool of spell work and is used to burn spell candles, incense, herbs, as well as to hold items to be blessed (usually for a period of 24 hours).

The bottom of the cauldron should be filled with earth from a sacred location; this can be from anywhere that the Witch feels is sacred, from an actual well-known sacred site (if it is permitted), to the seashore or place where the Witch was born. As with the knife, the Fairy Witch's cauldron must not be of iron but should be of an alternate material. A larger cauldron is preferred as it is used for so many different things; additionally, you may also choose to have a smaller secondary cauldron to use for certain spells that might require taking the cauldron out, while your main cauldron might be stationary on your altar.

The Quaich is a bowl with two handles used for drinking. It comes from Scotland and is associated with sharing drinks between friends or sweethearts; it is sometimes used in weddings. In Fairy Witchcraft the quaich is used as a symbol of the friendship between the Witch and the fairies and is the vessel which holds offerings of food and drink. A wooden bowl may be substituted if a Quaich can't be found. The Quaich can be decorated to the witch's taste.

Working with herbs and creating one's own incenses, teas, and charms is a common practice in Fairy Witchcraft and the mortar and pestle are essential for that. This tool represents the link between the Witch and the plant world and is a tool of transformation and healing. Ideally at least two mortar and pestles should be kept, one for making incenses and one for teas and medicinal herbs. It's important to keep your mortar and pestle clean and not use one for anything you will consume that has had poisonous material in it, so I suggest choosing different styles or materials that are easily differentiated.

The broom, ideally made of ash, birch and willow, is used to cleanse and bless ritual space. The ash represents the connection between the worlds. The birch represents cleansing and new beginnings and the willow represents flexibility and healing. The three together combine to energetically renew and refresh an area. Brooms can also be used in certain types of magic, including cleansings and banishings.

Through The Veil – Fairy Gifts

Part of being a Fairy Witch is always being aware of the energy around you and staying open to possibilities. Many times fairies will reach out to us and leave us gifts, but it is up to us to be able to recognize these gifts when we see them and be able to properly honor them. Many people have lived their whole lives being told not to trust their intuition and it can be very hard to re-learn this skill. Yet it is essential because a fairy gift offered once may never be offered again. In order to truly live as a Fairy Witch one must walk the line between mundane reality and magical awareness, and to some degree this is a matter of being open to perceiving the magic that is always around us.

While I was writing this book I was concerned about how open I should be and how much I should reveal. I came home one day and as I walked across my front lawn the wind picked up and the air filled with pink flower petals. Although I've lived in this house for decades nothing like this has ever happened before. The air filled with swirling flowers and a feeling of enchantment, as if just for a moment the rest of the world fell away. I could have ignored it but instead I embraced the moment as a gift.

Magic is all around us if we only slow down enough to see it.

Chapter 4

Basic Practice

Every religion must have its holy places, affording a means of communication between man, Gods, spirits, and forces of nature.
Hilda Ellis Davidson

At its most basic, sacred space is a special area or space that is set aside for worship or a natural place that provides a special connection to Powers beyond ourselves. Sacred space may be created or exist temporarily or permanently. Additionally, the formation of sacred space may be based in an acknowledgement of a place's inherent sacredness, such as we see in the Celtic practice of worshiping in groves of trees or by sacred wells, or may be an entirely human construct where a specific area is declared sacred or made sacred through ritual actions.

Within Fairy Witchcraft it is important to be able to recognize natural sacred spaces and connect to the spirits of place that exist there. When possible the Witch should find an outdoor sacred space near his or her home that can be used for worship. However, it is equally important to create a sacred space within the home. This place will act as a connection point with the fairies, ancestors, and the Gods and as the focal point of magical workings. Over time it becomes a place of power for the Witch.

Sometimes permanent, sometimes transitory, the altar is often the focal point of worship, a place we can connect to our Gods in an active way. A place to go when we need something to focus on, and a place that can act as a base for ritual. This idea is certainly not unique to neo-pagans; one look at the ancient temples of Greece, Rome, or Egypt show us that altars go hand in hand with many religions. In Fairy Witchcraft the altar is both a place of worship and also a place of magic, which is why we call it a working altar. The working altar is the central focus for the Fairy Witch and contains his or her tools, representations of deities, symbols of the three realms, as well as anything else the Witch needs to work or worship.

How you set up your altar is up to you. The important thing is that it creates a place for you to hold your rites and work your spells. I put my God and Goddess statues, tokens of my ancestors and the fairies, dried plants that I connect to and any other object that doesn't get handled much towards the back of the altar space. The mortar and pestle sit off to the right as does the Quaich. On the left I have a large raw amethyst and a small incense burner. A shell, stone and feather represent the three realms and my connection to them. My cauldron, which is bronze, sits in the center because it is the focal point of all my magical work; my wand and knife are placed to each side of the cauldron and my fairy stone is in front of it. Additionally, I have a Faery Oracle deck and an altar paten that I made which has a design of three oak leaves on it. My broom leans against one side. I have found this set-up works well for me whether I am honoring the Gods or fairies, or working magic. I encourage any Witch to experiment and find what works for him or her.

Beyond the Witch's working altar, one thing I always suggest to anyone interested in honoring the energy of Faery is to create a fairy altar. This can be as simple as a collection of found natural objects, or as elaborate as you can imagine. Fairies love pretty, shiny things, natural objects, crystals, flowers and (oddly) broken objects such as chipped coffee cups or broken statues. The only purpose of such an altar is to make the gesture of welcoming them into your home and providing a place to leave out offerings for them, which can either be in the house or outside in your yard. It is best to trust your instinct on this, no matter how nonsensical it seems, and allow the altar to grow naturally over time as it continues to accumulate more items. Mine has gotten rather elaborate at this point! It is up to the Witch whether to make this a separate altar or to combine this with the working altar.

In addition to the fairy altar it is a good idea to have a small altar or area set aside for the ancestors. This can be a true altar or simply a collection of pictures of the Witch's loved ones who have passed. Our ancestors are always with us and have a strong interest in our well-being, so it is wise to acknowledge and appreciate them. If you don't know who your ancestors are or have problems connecting emotionally to your immediate family you can use more generic representations of the ancestors such as skulls to create this connection. Otherwise it is up to you how simple or elaborate you make the space. Mine includes pictures of my deceased family members as well as a few objects owned by some of them, candles, an incense holder, a decorated skull to represent the ancestors whose names I do not know, and a deck of oracle cards. As with the fairy altar you might choose to incorporate the ancestor altar into your main working altar.

Circle casting is not used in offerings or spell work nor is it seen as necessary in most rituals of Fairy Witchcraft, but it can be used in more elaborate rituals and can be helpful in rituals to contact Faery directly. The purpose of casting the circle is to create an opening to the Otherworld within your ritual space. Be aware though that shifting your ritual space in this way can have some interesting effects; it is very common for time to be distorted and appear to either slow down or speed up, sometimes drastically.

The five elements of the Earth realm – air, fire, water, earth, and spirit – are used to anchor the circle and give it stability. They are invoked first, and then the circle itself is cast and the gateway opened. When the ritual is ended the process is reversed. It is very important to understand before doing this, that this is not a neo-pagan circle whose purpose would be to protect the caster from outside influences or contain raised energy. A fairy circle is an opening connecting to the Otherworld, and should not be done lightly. They can be used for rituals like self-dedications, for spiritual journeywork, or for casting major enchantments.

If you are working indoors, before casting the circle take the broom and walk three times sunwise around the space. Sweep with strong motions outwards while chanting or singing a simple blessing, such as:

Bless this space
Bless this place
Three times round
This blessing's bound.

To cast the circle start in the east.

Facing east, raise your hands and envision a strong wind blowing. Say:

Element of Air, Power of the East,
I call you attend this circle
To guard me in my rite
Join me now!

Turn to the south, raise your hands, envision a roaring fire, and say:

Element of Fire, Power of the South,
I call you attend this circle
To guard me in my rite
Join me now!

Turn to the west, raise your hands, envision a driving rain, and say:

Element of Water, Power of the West,
I call you attend this circle
To guard me in my rite
Join me now!

Turn to the north, raise your hands, envision fresh turned earth, and say:

Element of Earth, Power of the North,
I call you attend this circle
To guard me in my rite
Join me now!

Finally, stand in front of your altar, raise your hands, and open your heart. Say:

Element of Spirit, Power of the Center,
I call you attend this circle
To guard me in my rite
Join me now!

After calling the elements, pick up your ritual knife. Starting in the east, walk the perimeter of your ritual area, visualizing the blade cutting a line of energy which expands into a sphere surrounding you. When you have completed the circuit, return to your altar. Set the knife down. Clearly and strongly say:

I stand now between the worlds
Where time is timeless
I stand now between the worlds
Where mortal earth and Faery join
I stand now between the worlds
Where wish and will unite

Once the circle is cast, you want to invite the fairy folk but this has to be done with extreme caution. It's important to extend the invitation because this is one of the ways that alliances and friendships with the fairies are built, but you must be careful not to invite in faeries that want to do you harm or are dangerous. Say:

I welcome all goodly inclined friendly spirits.

Now perform the body of your rite. This can include calling in the ancestors and the Gods as well as different acts of magic or prayers and offerings. When finished, stand before your altar and say:

To all goodly inclined spirits who joined me here, may there be peace and friendship between us.

Then say:

The doorway to Faery is closed
The flow of time returns
The doorway to Faery is closed
I stand again on mortal earth
The doorway to Faery is closed
As I will it, so it is.

Walk the boundary of your space again with ritual knife, this time seeing the energy returning into the blade. When done, stand before your altar again and put your ritual knife down. Lower your head slightly and say:

Element of Spirit, Power of the Center,
I release you from this circle
In peace and power.

Offer some of the energy from the ritual to the elemental spirit. Turn to the east, lower your head slightly and say:

Element of Air, Power of the East,
I release you from this circle
In peace and power.

Offer some of the energy from the ritual to the elemental spirit. Turn to the south, lower your head slightly and say:

Element of Fire, Power of the South,
I release you from this circle
In peace and power.

Offer some of the energy from the ritual to the elemental spirit. Turn to the west, lower your head slightly and say:

Element of Water, Power of the West,
I release you from this circle
In peace and power.

Offer some of the energy from the ritual to the elemental spirit. Turn to the north, lower your head slightly and say:

Element of Earth, Power of the North,
I release you from this circle
In peace and power.

After taking down the circle it is essential to be sure you ground your energy. Eat and drink something, lay out flat on the earth or on the floor if you are inside, or put a small amount of salt on your tongue.

Through The Veil – A Fairy Tale

Once there was a man named Thomas and as he sat on a river bank one day he saw a rider coming up through a grove of elder trees. The woman rode a shining white horse and bells hung from the horse's bridle and rang out with each step. The woman herself was wearing a green dress the color of fresh grown grass and she was beautiful beyond anyone Thomas had ever seen before. As she drew closer he greeted her and called her a Goddess, but she corrected him: 'I am the Queen of Fairyland, Thomas, and I have come to take you with me.'

She told him that he must serve her in Fairyland for seven years, and took him up onto her horse then rode away. They passed across rivers and into a land where neither sun nor moon shone down, and this was the land of Fairy where she ruled. She offered Thomas an apple to eat and told him that once he ate it he would be able to predict the future, then he was given green clothes to wear and set to serve the Fairy Queen.

It seemed that only hours had passed when he was told that his seven years was up and he should return to mortal earth. Once there he found that he could speak prophecy in rhyme and he came to be called 'True Thomas' because he spoke truly of the future, and he was called 'Thomas the Rhymer' because he spoke his prophecy in rhyme. He became famous far and wide.

When Thomas was an old man the Queen of Fairyland returned and told him it was time for him to go, and he was never seen again on mortal earth.

Chapter 5

Prayer, Invocations, and Offerings

Prayer is a way for us to speak to the Gods and it's important to do so regularly. Anyone can pray, all it takes is a genuine heart and sincere words. Prayer can be used to praise the Gods or to ask for or thank the Gods for blessings, or to ask for protection. For example:

Bless, O Gods 10
Bless, O generous Gods,
Myself and everything near me,
Bless me in all my actions,
May I be safe for ever,
May I be safe for ever.
From every brownie and bansidhe,
From every evil wish and sorrow,
From every nymph and water-wraith,
From every fairy-mouse and grass-mouse,
From every fairy-mouse and grass-mouse.
From every troll among the hills,
From every siren hard pressing me,
From every ghoul within the glens,
Oh! save me till the end of my days.
Oh! save me till the end of my days.

This short little prayer adapted from the *Carmina Gadelica* is an excellent one for daily protection for the Fairy Witch, and might also be used in an emergency situation if 'under the strong shield of your protection' was added onto the end of the 4th and 5th lines. There are many examples of traditional prayers like this in the Fairy Faith that can be used, but you can also write your own easily enough. The important thing is to have a clear intent. For example, a prayer I use every day for the Fairy Goddess Macha is:

Macha, woman of the Sidhe,
Battle Goddess, Red-haired Queen,
Skilled in magic, great in power, full in knowledge,
Guide my feet on my path, as I honor the old wisdom
Guide my hands in offering, as I honor the old Gods
Guide my heart in strength, as I honor the old ways.

Prayers can also be used to ask for protection from things like storms, such as in this one that I use when hurricanes or blizzards hit the area I live in:

Prayer of Protection Against Storms
Protect, O mighty Gods,
Myself and everything near me,
My family and my home,
May we be safe through the storm,
may we be safe through the storm
From every gust and gale,
From every flood and downpour,
From every tide and storm surge,
Through the day and darkest night,
through the day and darkest night.
From every tree whose roots give way,
From every branch that breaks,
From every danger seen and unseen,
Shield us and keep us from harm
oh, shield us and keep us from harm!
(if desired this can be added as well)
The keeping of the Gods of Power on us
The keeping of Danu always on us,

The keeping of Lugh and Dagda on us,
The keeping of the three Morrigan on us
And the keeping of Nuada the silver-armed on us
King Nuada the silver-armed on us
The keeping of Brighid and Airmed on us
The keeping of all the Gods of Power
The keeping of the People of peace
The keeping of land, sea, and sky
And the ancestors watching over us
and the ancestors watching over us.

In many traditional Fairy Faith cultures prayers were sung or chanted and this is still a good way to do them. Singing or chanting makes the words easier to remember and also creates an automatic flow of energy. Not only is it perfectly acceptable to make up your own, but it is also fun and they don't need to be complicated or overly wordy.

In a similar vein, besides prayer, a practitioner of Fairy Witchcraft should also have a firm grasp of the use of invocations. Whereas prayer is a way to talk to the Powers and express gratitude or ask for protection or blessing, invocation is done to call them to you, especially in ritual, although invocation may also be used during offerings and some types of magic. Invoking the Gods is done by calling to them, using descriptive terms, and asking them to be present. For example:

Lady of the Greenwood, Flower of Spring,
Who ripens fruit and quickens life,
Join us as we dance and sing
And celebrate in your name.

As with prayer, this is best done in song when possible, but can be chanted or spoken as well. It doesn't need to rhyme, of course, just to create an image for you of the deity being invoked. As you sing or say the words, visualize the deity you are calling. Invocations should be tailored to the circumstances, so when calling on a Goddess for healing you want to mention those qualities.

Invoking your ancestors can be done by simply calling their names, by describing something about them, or by saying something like:

I call to my ancestors,
Those who have gone before
Flesh and blood and bone
My kin across the veil
Join me here in my rite
Be with me as I honor you.

As I previously mentioned, when invoking the faeries you want to be careful to be very clear that you are only inviting in the ones that mean you no harm. Although this will still open you up to mischief, it is the safest approach. It is very unwise to simply put out a blanket invitation to anything that might feel like dropping by. Any time you are dealing with fairies there is an inherent danger, so a Fairy Witch must be cautious and wise in what she or he does and how it is done.

Offerings to all the Powers that the Witch honors should be made regularly. This can include the fairies, ancestors, and Gods. You can pray when you make an offering or simply meditate on the connection you are trying to form and strengthen. As with prayer, one of the most important aspects of offerings is a sincere heart. The point of making offerings is to establish reciprocity between yourself and the Power you are offering to; the more often you offer, the stronger the connection grows.

You should always offer the best of whatever you have to offer – remember the fairies hate a stingy person. While spontaneous offerings are always fine, it's a good idea to decide on a schedule of regular offerings as well. At the least this should be on the eight holidays, but you may choose to also make offerings on the full moon as well. I offer to the fairies once a week. Remember though that once you commit to any regular schedule of offerings it's important to keep to that schedule unless it's absolutely impossible to do so. Under difficult circumstances you can always offer a song or poem.

What you offer will depend on who you are offering to. Generally, lighting candles, burning incense, poetry, energy or offering silver can be done to any Power. Different Gods from specific pantheons, like the Tuatha de Danann, often have certain offering preferences as do the liminal Gods. The Lady of the Greenwood and Lord of the Wildwood like offerings of fresh water and fruit, vegetables, or nuts, especially those you have grown yourself. The Hunter and the Queen of the Wind prefer offerings of skill, things you have made yourself, which can include anything from art or poetry to incense, or baked goods.

The fairies are usually offered fresh water, milk, cream, honey, porridge, candy, cookies, cakes, butter, fruit, or bread. Sometimes they may be offered silver, especially jewelry, as well as coins or crystals. I generally avoid offering alcohol or meat in almost all cases as these can attract the wrong sort of fairies or stir up wild energy. Keep in mind that once you start offering to them, if you suddenly stop or reduce the quality of the offerings they may decide to take it anyway, usually in an excessive and dramatic fashion. At one point in my life, for example, my income suddenly decreased and I become a bit worried about having enough for the family, so I stopped offering the fairies milk (although I kept offering other things). The second week after making this decision, on the day I would normally offer, I was unloading groceries from my car when I had a gallon of milk pulled from my hand; it struck the ground and burst. After that I made sure to offer a bit of milk every time.

With the ancestors, generally, lighting a candle for those you love who have passed on and leaving a bit of coffee or tea on your ancestor altar (if you have one) or pouring some out onto the earth is a good way to go. I have found that the ancestors often want little more than your attention – to be spoken to and acknowledged.

Offerings should be made with proper respect, as if you are giving a gift to a good friend. If outdoors, be sure what you are giving won't harm the environment. If indoors, leave the item on your altar for a day and then dispose of it; the Power receiving the item consumes its essence but leaves behind the physical object. Ideally liquids should be poured out onto the earth and solid items should be given to water or buried. It is important at outdoor sites not to create a large mess or leave behind any litter; remember that part of honoring fairies associated with a specific location is being respectful of the location itself.

Through The Veil – Rings and Things

One thing that is a common occurrence when fairies are around is items disappearing. Sometimes they re-appear fairly quickly, other times they may be missing for an extended period of time. A good indication that the disappearance is fairy related is if it was last seen in an obvious place (out in the open), the disappearance makes no sense, and the re-appearance also makes no sense; usually the item that goes missing is important in some way. It may be your car keys or a piece of jewelry for example. In the case of car keys, they are known to disappear from countertops only to re-appear in the exact same spot later.

Once I took off a garnet ring that had been given to me as a Mother's Day gift and set it down on a shelf in my living room. The next morning the ring was gone. I looked everywhere, even moving the book shelf, but it was nowhere to be found. After a few weeks of fruitless searching I gave up. Several months later I was reaching for some spare change on the center console of my car when my fingers brushed something that didn't feel like a coin. Looking over I saw my missing ring sitting there.

Another time I took off a bracelet that had been a gift from a good friend. When I went to put it back on it was gone and could not be found. Weeks later we moved from the house and I was certain I would never see it again, only to find it on the bathroom floor of the new house one morning shortly after moving in. This sort of thing is pretty common with anyone who deals often with fairies.

Chapter 6

Fairy Holidays

Just as there are specific liminal places where you are more likely to see fairy activity, there are certain times and certain days of the year that are especially associated with the fairies. These are often the in-between times: dawn and dusk, the transition points of the year, midnight. Celebrating the holidays in Fairy Witchcraft isn't just about holding a ritual in honor of the day, it is also about a series of devotional style acts that acknowledge the shifts in the energy and builds relationships with the fairies at these times. Fairy rituals are not rigidly set but rather organic rituals that require the Witch to be sensitive to the flow of energy. They follow a loose structure of invocation, prayer, offering, and thanks. If you don't make offerings at any other times, it's important to make them at these times. The eight holy days of Fairy Witchcraft are: Samhain, Midwinter solstice, Imbolc, Spring equinox, Beltane, Midsummer solstice, Lughnasa, and Autumn equinox; in addition, the full and dark moons are celebrated.

As in mainstream neo-paganism and Irish polytheism, Samhain is celebrated as the beginning of the New Year. It is also the end of summer and beginning of winter and the time when the rule of the liminal Gods changes from the Lady of the Greenwood and Lord of the Wildwood to the Hunter and Queen of the Wind. Samhain is celebrated as a three-day holiday beginning on the evening of October 31st. On this night the world of fairy is opened up and during this period the denizens of Faery are most likely to be encountered (Estyn Evans, 1957; McNeill, 1961). Historically, people would travel in groups to avoid being kidnapped into Faery and should a person meet a Fairy Rade at that time and throw the dust from the road at them they would be compelled to release anyone they had taken (Danaher, 1972).

In Fairy Witchcraft this is the time to visit and clean the graves of deceased loved ones and to light a candle in their memory. Food offerings may be left out for the wandering dead on the 31st and an offering of porridge or caudle should be left out for the fairies. On the second night of Samhain a ritual may be conducted for the liminal Gods to welcome back the Hunter and Queen of the Wind. A blessing prayer for the New Year can be said, and divination done for the year to come. Offerings should be left out for the Gods and spirits. On the final day of Samhain, November 2nd, the dead return to visit the living and they should be welcomed with a bowl of fresh water or an extra chair at the table (Estyn Evans, 1957; Danaher, 1972).

Midwinter solstice is a time of blessing the home and of omens. Holly, hazel, and rowan are hung up around the home and the entire house is fumigated with burning juniper. Juniper can be hard to find here in the United States, so I make an incense blend that includes juniper berries for the purpose of cleansing. On the eve of the solstice a silver coin is left out on the doorstep and if it is still there in the morning it is seen as a sign of prosperity for the year to come, but if it has gone, it's an ill omen.

Wearing new clothes on the solstice day is good luck as is carrying a silver coin in your pocket. To see a red dawn on the solstice means bad luck and strife to come and the direction of the wind is an omen of the year to come as well: 'Wind from the west, fish and bread, wind from the north, cold and flaying, wind from the east, snow on the hills, wind from the south, fruit on trees.' (McNeill, 1961, p. 115)

This is the time when the Wild Hunt is most active, gathering wandering souls and the unwary to bring across to the Spirit world. A Fairy Witch may choose to light candles for the wandering souls to help them find their way. This is the time when the dangerous fairies are the most active and offerings are made to the fairies, particularly to the Witch's fairy allies, for a year of peace and blessing. This is also the traditional time to make offerings to the house fairies; usually a thick porridge with a pat of butter on top is left out the night before the solstice for them.

In my own ritual practice I bake a cake in honor of the solstice and offer pieces to the fairies; the rest is shared among the family. The ritual focuses on the hope within the darkness of winter and the rebirth of the light. The Hunter and Queen of the Wind are prayed to for protection and safety during the winter months.

Imbolc, on February 2nd, is the next holiday. The main charms and talismans of Imbolc focus on cleansing and blessing. First, there is the Brighid's cross, a woven sun wheel shape which represents the cycle of the year and the four main holy days, according to the book *Apple Branch*. On Imbolc, you can weave new Brighid's crosses, or bless ones you already have, although it may be better to burn the old and weave new each year when possible. A Brighid's cross is protective and healing to have in the home.

A second talisman is the brídeóg, or 'little Brigid', a small cloth or straw doll wearing white clothes. In some cases, the brídeóg would be made from straw saved from the previous Lughnasa. This doll played a role in ritual after being brought outside, usually carried by the eldest daughter, then invited to enter the home where it was led with all ceremony to a specially prepared little bed. The doll was left in the bed overnight and its presence was believed to bless all those in the household.

Another talisman connected to Imbolc is Brigid's mantle, or 'an brat Bríd', a length of cloth left out on the window sill over the course of the holy day and night. It is believed that this cloth can be used for healing and protection throughout the year. This talisman would be kept and recharged every year, attaining full power after seven years.

The ritual on Imbolc centers on cleansing. Before the ritual, the home and ritual area should be cleaned as thoroughly as possible. In the ritual the Witch should ceremonially wash her hands as an act of cleansing and to prepare her for the work of the year to come. This is the best time for dedication rituals and to bless tools for magical use.

It is said that the fairies move their houses, from one hill to another, at the equinoxes. The Spring equinox is a good time to focus on the things that you intend to plant and nourish in your own life in the coming growing season. It is a time of balance and renewal of the earth. Offerings should be left outside for the faeries. The Witch should use this time of year to ritually set intentions of things to grow or goals for the next six months. An excellent way to do this is to choose three colors of thread or yarn that represent your goal and, in ritual, weave them together to form a talisman that can be worn or kept on the altar.

The fairies were thought to be especially active and powerful on Beltane and for the first three days of May. Beltane was another day when the fairies moved from one hill to another and this meant they were more likely to cause mischief or steal people, particularly babies, brides, midwives, and musicians (Danaher, 1972). Primrose was scattered across doorways to protect the household from the fairies stealing the family's luck, herbs, or milk (Wilde, 1991). Fairies might travel disguised as humans trying to borrow a bit of milk or fire, and if a person was foolish enough to lend it they would lose their luck for the year. Small pieces of iron or bits of rowan might be carried for protection by those who feared the fairies' mischief. (Danaher, 1972).

Rowan is seen as the best protection against the fairies and at Beltane rowan branches were collected and hung up around the home, or tied with red thread and hung up over the door (McNeill, 1959). In Ireland, the rowan is believed to be the best of all protections against bad luck and enchantment, so on May Day morning a branch of rowan might be woven into the ceiling to protect the house and all within it for the next year (Danaher, 1972).

In Laois, Ireland, there was a tradition where the head of the household would light a candle and then go around the house blessing the door, hearth, four corners of the home, and each family member from eldest to youngest before placing a rowan branch in the house (Danaher, 1972). In Fairy Witchcraft, rowan might be collected on Beltane eve and used to make protective charms for the year to come. This is the time when the home is blessed; as in the ceremony described above, the Witch would take a candle and walk her property and home praying for blessing by singing (or saying):

People of peace,
Bless our home, bless our family;
Keep hate and curses away from us,
Bring to us luck and prosperity,
Bless us now on Beltane.

This is also the time when the rule of the liminal Gods switches from the Hunter and Queen of the Wind to the Lady of the Greenwood and Lord of the Wildwood, as the year turns form the dark half to the light half, from winter to summer. It is a holiday that celebrates fertility of the earth and its inhabitants and any child conceived on Beltane has special luck and a connection to Faery. A ritual for Beltane can focus on welcoming back the Lady of the Greenwood and Lord of the Wildwood and rejoicing in the spark of new life in the world.

The Midsummer solstice is a time of magic and enchantment. On the shortest night of the year the fairies tend to be very active but also at their most friendly; you have the best chance of meeting a benign fairy now, although if you are on the receiving end of their mischief you may not feel that it is harmless. Offerings of flowers, cakes, and cookies are made and ritual focuses on joy and celebration using music and dance.

Lughnasa, on August 2nd, is the beginning of the harvest. It is a time to visit and decorate holy wells and standing stones (MacNeill, 1962). If you do not live near any you can still go visit your own local sacred sites or locations you associate with particular fairies and decorate these places. Remember that the location should be approached and circled three times sunwise, for blessing, before entering and that any decorations you bring should be biodegradable and safe for wildlife. Bread can be baked and either dipped in honey or drizzled with it and then some can be offered to the fairies, ancestors, and Gods and the rest eaten by the family or individual. Divination focusing on weather during the coming months was traditionally practiced (Danaher, 1972).

The Autumn equinox, like the Spring equinox, is a time of transition as the energy shifts and is also a time when the fairies move their homes from hill to hill. Now is the time to reflect on the goals that were set in the spring and also to look at what things in your life – habits, patterns, relationships – you are ready to let go of. These things should be listed and burned in ritual.

Besides these holidays, Fairy Witchcraft also celebrates the full and dark moon each month. These represent the liminal points in the month when the energy shifts from light to dark and dark to light. Honoring these times allows the Witch to better connect to Fairy and also to regularly exercise his or her own skills.

The full moon is the best time for all magics and to make talismans and charms. Ritual would be aimed at honoring the Gods of the light half of the year, the Lady of the Greenwood and Lord of the Wildwood, and also for ritually acknowledging and expressing gratitude for the blessings in the Witch's life. You may also choose to make offerings to the fairies and the ancestors.

The new moon is the best time for divination and for journey work to communicate with Faery. Ritual honors the Gods of the dark half of the year, the Hunter and the Queen of the Wind. This is also the best time for making ritual tools and for baneful magic, including banishings, bindings, and hexing.

Through The Veil – Midsummer Moth

I used to co-run a spiritual discussion group with a friend out of a store she owns and one year we held a midsummer ritual. The group's energy that night was joyous and gentle; after ritual, people stayed to chat and the front door was opened to let in some fresh air. As I stood talking with my friend who owned the store and another mutual friend, suddenly a large pale shape flew in the door and hovered by the ceiling. My friend saw a huge white moth. Both our mutual friend and I saw a small, ugly man with moth-like wings.

The fairy looked at us and we looked at him, and then my friend wondered out loud how we'd get it out of the store. Our mutual friend threw up his hand, pointing at the little fairy, and sternly said 'You!' Instantly the being plummeted down into a front window display and disappeared. Literally disappeared, as my friend searched for the 'moth' in vain for several minutes, despite the fact that there was nowhere in that area for anything that size to hide.

Chapter 7

Fairy Plants and Animals

All plants have spirits, but some plants in particular are associated with fairies or with use in Witchcraft. These include (but are not limited to) bluebells, yarrow, tansy, foxglove, violets, pansy, ragweed, shamrock, primrose, and mushrooms, as well as many types of trees, but especially hawthorn and blackthorn.

It's important for any Witch to have at least a basic understanding of the uses of plants, but for the Fairy Witch it is also important to nurture a relationship with the spirit of both the individual plant and that type of plant as a whole. The best way to do this is to choose one or two that grow wild near you, or always seem to be around you, and begin getting to know the plant. Research its historic and modern uses as well as magic associated with it. Simultaneously spend some time with the living plant; meditate next to it, talk to it, leave it offerings. Ask the spirit of the plant to communicate with you and be open to responses. Not every plant will respond with equal strength, but over time you should be able to create a relationship with the plant and its spirit. When you have created a connection to the plant and you feel that it is something you want to continuously have, you can ask the plant if it is willing to partner with you; if the answer is yes, harvest a small amount to dry and keep on your altar. Keep in mind that you should never harvest any magical plant with an iron blade or tool as this will destroy the plant's spirit. Working magic with plants with which you have created this connection will give you stronger and longer lasting results.

It's beyond the scope of this book to cover every herb that a Fairy Witch could work with, but I will use yarrow and shamrock as examples of how to approach researching and using these plants. This same basic approach can be used with any fairy herb or tree. As with anything medical please consult a doctor or certified herbalist before using any of the following herbs to treat any conditions. The *Carmina Gadelica* has a variety of charms relating to specific herbs. These charms are useful to anyone who in modern practice uses herbs either medicinally or magically, so I will include some of them here by discussing the charms as I use them with the herb's properties.

Yarrow

Yarrow is probably one of my favorite herbs to work with, magically. Lady Wilde tells us that it is an excellent magical herb and was sown into clothing to impart its properties to the wearer (Wilde, 1991). She also mentions an Irish folk charm where ten yarrow leaves are plucked and nine placed in your sock for protection, with the tenth given as an offering to the spirits (Wilde, 1991). Yarrow can be associated with protection, love, beauty, and healing; its scientific name, achillea millefolium, is from its association with the Greek hero Achilles who was said to use it on the battlefield to treat injured soldiers.

Yarrow features in two charms in Volume 2 of the *Carmina Gadelica*, which are intended to make the bearer more attractive and to protect from heart-ache. Interestingly in lines 7 through 10 of the first charm, the woman associates herself with sea, land, sky and the tree, before declaring her strength and dominance. The following are my versions, based on the originals.

The Yarrow 163
I will pluck the yarrow fair,
That my face shall be more gentle,
That my lips shall be more warm,
That my speech shall be more chaste,
My speech will be the beams of the sun,
My lips will be the juice of the strawberry.

May I be an isle in the sea,
May I be a hill on the shore,
May I be a star in the waning of the moon,
May I be a staff to the weak,
I can wound every man,
No man can wound me.
Excerpt from By Land, Sea, and Sky

The Yarrow 164
I will pluck the yarrow fair,
That more brave shall be my hand,
That more warm shall be my lips,
That more swift shall be my foot;
May I be an island at sea,
May I be a rock on land,
That I can afflict any man,
Yet no man can afflict me.
Excerpt from By Land, Sea, and Sky

Although large doses are toxic, small amounts of yarrow tea can be used for internal bleeding, indigestion, colds, fevers, and to increase appetite (Foster & Duke, 2000). Yarrow can be applied externally as a poultice to stop bleeding and has a long history of being used for this in both Europe and America (Foster & Duke, 2000). The plant can be found wild in fields and near roads, growing about 3 feet tall with clusters of tiny white flowers (Foster & Duke, 2000). Yarrow can also be grown in gardens and is easily dried by hanging.

Shamrock

The *Carmina Gadelica* includes two charms about the shamrock (Seamrog or 'little clover' in Irish) which could include any species of trefoil, although there is debate over which trefoil exactly was originally being referenced. The most likely candidates seem to be red or white clover or lesser clover, all of which are known as shamrocks in different areas of Ireland and Scotland.

Medicinally, shamrock has a long history of use. Historically it was used as an anti-spasmodic in the treatment of bronchitis and whooping cough (Grieve, 1971). It may also have been used in poultices to treat cancerous tumors (Grieve, 1971). Red clover is still used medicinally today as an anti-spasmodic and anti-tumor, as well as a diuretic, expectorant, and stimulant (DeVries, 2010). White clover in America has a long medicinal use as well, externally treating skin disorders, gout symptoms, and eye problems, and is used in a tea for fevers and coughs (Plant Life, 2012). Because there are multiple types of trefoils that are called shamrocks, anyone seeking to use them medicinally needs to clearly identify which exact type of clover they are dealing with and research its unique medicinal properties before using it.

Magically, shamrocks are best known for bringing good luck, and in Fairy Witchcraft it is believed to aid the second sight, or ability to see fairies and other spirits. Additionally, modern magical practitioners use them for success, money, protection, love, and fidelity (Cunningham, 1985). When utilizing the traditional charms from the *Carmina Gadelica* for shamrocks, one might also add peace, fertility, and health to its magical uses. For that purpose you would want to chant the charm over the plant while harvesting it and save it for later use or carry it with you to gain its effect.

Below are my updated pagan versions of the traditional shamrock charms. Charm #170 is meant to be used with lucky clovers which may have four or five leaves, depending on which school of thought the person follows, as some say that four leaves are lucky and others favor five. From page 106 of Volume 2 of the *Carmina Gadelica* 'some people say that the lucky shamrock has four leaves, other say five, but all agree it must be found by chance not sought out intentionally. Once found it is preserved as a peerless talisman.' (Carmichael, 1900). The charm references seven joys, including health, friends, cattle, sheep, children, peace and piety, all of which are magnified by possessing a lucky four (or five) leaf shamrock.

Lucky Shamrock Charm 170
Shamrock of good omens,
Beneath the bank growing
On which stood the gracious Lugh,
the many-skilled God.
The seven joys are,
Without evil traces,
On you, peerless one
Of the sunbeams–
Joy of health,
Joy of friends,
Joy of cattle,
Joy of sheep,
Joy of sons, and
Daughters fair,
Joy of peace,
Joy of the Gods!
The four leaves of the straight stem, (alternately five)
Of the straight stem from the root of the hundred rootlets,
You shamrock of promise,
you are bounty and blessing at all times.

Alternately, for those of us without cattle or sheep, there is this more heavily re-written version:

Shamrock of good omens,
Beneath the bank growing
On which stood the gracious Lugh,
the many-skilled God.

The seven joys are,
Without evil traces,
On you, peerless one
Of the sunbeams—
Joy of health,
Joy of friends,
Joy of prosperity
Joy of abundance,
Joy of fertility, and
Success fair,
Joy of peace,
Joy of the Gods!
The four leaves of the straight stem, (alternately five)
Of the straight stem from the root of the hundred rootlets,
You shamrock of promise,
you are bounty and blessing at all times.

This next short charm is rather ambiguous in its meaning and could apply to any type of clover. It seems to me to imply both a protective quality to the shamrock and an association with the dead. It may also mean that shamrocks are good to plant on graves.

Shamrock of Power Charm 171
Shamrock of foliage,
Shamrock of power,
Shamrock of foliage,
Which Airmed found under the bank,
Shamrock of my love,
Of most beautiful hue,
I would choose you in death,
To grow on my grave,
I would choose you in death,
To grow on my grave

Animals

As there are certain plants that are associated with fairies and which have a spirit of their own, there are also certain types of fairies that take on the appearance of or chiefly have the form of certain animals. Fairy animals are themselves fairies and have an intelligence beyond what we would expect from their shape. Often fairy animals appear missing a limb or ears, or are otherwise deformed. You may meet fairy animals in our world or when in the Otherworld and it is important to have a basic understanding of what to expect and that they are fairies, no matter what they look like on the outside.

Swans

A swan should never be harmed as swans are not always what they appear to be; there is a long standing prohibition in the Fairy Faith against killing swans. Swans may be fairies or may be people transformed by magic into the form of swans.

Fairy Hounds

Fairy hounds can appear in several ways: as lean white hounds with red ears, as large black dogs, or as shaggy greenish-furred dogs. Some people believe that seeing a fairy hound is an omen of death, particularly when it is the large black dog which is sighted.

Fairy Cows

Fairy cows are water fairies that usually live in lakes. They appear as young hornless white heifers which emerge from the lake to graze on the shore and then return to the waters. Fairy cows often attend to or belong to lake maidens, a type of lake fairy.

Fairy Horses

There are several types of fairy horse but the ones most often spoken of are the Water Horse, Kelpie, and Puca. Each appears as a dark shaggy horse, usually friendly and willing to be ridden, but if a person is foolish enough to climb on the back of a fairy horse, the fairy will take off on a wild ride. If the person is lucky they will have mounted a Puca who will eventually throw them in a ditch, but if it is a Kelpie or water horse they may be taken to a body of water, drowned, and eaten. The Puca is also able to take the form of a dark-haired man, black dog, or goat and is known to make mischief; all the fruit left on the tree after Samhain belongs to the fairies as it is believed the Puca urinates on it after Samhain night. The Kelpie is a bit more ambiguous and can be dangerous, but has also been known to develop connections to certain people. The Water Horse, however, is generally dangerous and should be avoided or treated with great care.

Fairy Deer
Fairy deer are usually white and often hinds (female deer). They can appear to lead you along your way but may also be fairies transformed.

Fairy Cats
In Irish and Scottish folklore there exist stories about cat sidhe (fairy cats) also called cat sith in Scottish Gaelic. Sidhe and sith are both pronounced 'shee'. Cat sidhe are believed to be large, Otherworldly black cats with a single white spot on the chest. These cats are generally seen as malevolent and some people believe they are actually shape-changed Witches. In particular, the Witch was believed to be able to transform into a cat nine times, but legend says on the ninth time the Witch would have to remain a cat forever (Old Farmer's Almanac, 2012). Jane Manning has a lovely children's book called *Cat Nights* based on this legend that both of my girls love, about a young Witch who has adventures each night as a cat for eight nights and then has to decide if she wants to stay a person or transform one last time. It is also said by some within the MacGillivray family that the clan motto

'Touch not this cat' is based on the family having a cat sidhe among its ancestors (MacGillivray, 2000).

Others believe that these cats are dangerous fairies that should be avoided. In Scotland it is believed that the cat sidhe can steal the souls of the newly dead and so certain protections must be undertaken while the body was watched until burial (MacGillivray, 2000). Most of these protections depend on doing things to distract the cat sidhe and keep it away from the body, such as sprinkling cat nip about the other rooms, or playing games that would draw the cat sidhe's attention (MacGillivray, 2000).

Through The Veil – Fairy Hounds

I have seen fairy hounds twice in my life.

The first time, many years ago, a friend and I were trying to cleanse and protect a mutual friend's business in the city. We sat in the doorway with a small cauldron and burned herbs, the smoke rising into the darkness of the early evening sky. Suddenly we both became aware of the eerie silence – the sounds of the city had fallen away, the traffic had stopped going past on the street, everything seemed deserted. As we watched, two huge black dogs came trotting down the side walk across the street. No one was with them, but they walked calmly and with a purpose.

My friend broke the silence and joked that perhaps they would cross the (empty) street, and no sooner had the words left his mouth when both dogs changed directions and moved across the street towards us. We immediately fled into the building and closed the door; peering out the window, we looked to watch the dogs walk past and saw nothing. Literally no dogs, anywhere. Venturing back out, there were no dogs to be seen in any direction, even though there was nowhere they could have gone in that amount of time. Moments later, the sound and traffic returned.

The second time I saw a faery hound happened when I was working as an EMT. My partner and I were on a layover at 5am on a winter morning in a city by the shore of Long Island Sound and we had parked in a lot next to a large field fenced off for construction. My partner was reading a book but I decided to get out and stretch my legs while we waited, despite the cold weather. I walked over near the chain-link fence that surrounded that field and noticed something white moving on the far side.

As I watched in the darkness the white shape moved steadily towards me; it seemed to be moving quickly across the field and eventually I realized it was a dog although its gait seemed odd. I looked past it for any sign of a person out for a morning walk with their pet but saw no one. The white dog, some sort of hound by its shape, was so white that it almost glowed in the pre-dawn darkness and I stood there watching it come straight towards me, trying to puzzle out why it was alone in a fenced in field and why its movement seemed jerky and off even though it moved quickly.

When it had crossed about two-thirds of the space between us I finally realized that it had only one front leg – not that it was missing one, but that its front leg was placed in the center of its chest. A wave of fear went over me and before I could think I had turned, run, and jumped back into the ambulance. My partner looked up, startled, and asked me what was wrong, and I told him there was a dog. Looking out he asked me what dog. Sure enough when I looked there was no dog to be seen anywhere, despite the fact that there was nowhere for it to go and no time for it to have gone anywhere.

Chapter 8

Fairy Familiars, Guides, and Communicating with the Otherworld

It is essential for the Fairy Witch to have fairies that are willing to guide and protect the person in their practice. This is not a simple matter though, nor is it something that will happen quickly. Eventually you will find one or two plant spirits that speak very strongly to you and you can ask if those plants are willing to be your plant familiars, and that's a step in the right in direction. The fairy familiar is a more difficult matter and is something that will come to the Witch in its own time. There are some who say that the fairy familiar is a gift sent to the Witch from the Queen of Fairyland, while others say that the familiar is a fairy that chooses to serve the Witch of its own free will.

The fairy familiar is not at all like the common modern idea of a familiar, which often more closely resembles a beloved pet, nor is it like the demonic familiars described during the Witch hysteria. Fairy familiars do have a physical, tangible form in our world and appear to the Witch offering aid in helping them in life. Usually this is done through the familiar giving advice that, if followed, allows the Witch to live comfortably and securely. Often the fairy familiar also helps the Witch in her healing work and divination and may act as a go-between for the Witch and other fairies.

It may be many years, if ever, before a Fairy Witch has a fairy familiar come to him or her, but it is still possible to make allies with fairies to help you in your practice. This can be done with local fairies by making offerings to them and reaching out in friendship. It can also be done in the Otherworld during spiritual journeys, and in fact it is important to have a fairy who agrees to be your ally and guide there.

Practicing Fairy Witchcraft is reliant upon several things, including the use of techniques that open the Witch up to the Otherworld. These can include divination, trance work, guided meditations, and spiritual journeys. For people with absolutely no experience in these areas I highly recommend reading Diana Paxson's book *Trance-Portation* before attempting to do any active journey work.

The most basic form of communication is divination which can be accomplished in a variety of ways. I prefer Brian Froud's The Faeries' Oracle deck but there are now several different fairy oracles to choose from as well as some tarot decks that can work. I find that tarot is often too structured and rigid for fairy work, but if you simply throw down cards without using a set spread then it is possible. The purpose, of course, is to open a line of communication with the fairies that live in your home, your immediate area, and who are willing to be your allies. You can try to use divination tools with other fairies as well, but like a telephone, it will only work if the party receiving the call is willing to pick up and answer.

Trance work, which may include dancing, singing, labyrinth walking, or anything else that will induce a trance state, opens the Witch up to a deeper level of awareness. This in turn can allow the person to perceive communication from spirits that the person is usually blind and deaf to. Trance work requires practice and should be done with a partner at first for safety.

Guided mediations are another option to allow the Witch to open him or herself up to communication. When working with a group, one person would read through the body of the meditation while everyone else experiences what is being described; when working alone the Witch must memorize the outline of the meditation and be able to follow it while going through it. This can be challenging. One must also learn to differentiate between messages from your own mind and those from outside, which can take time and practice.

The final means of communication is the spiritual journey, where the Witch sends his or her spirit out to travel to the Otherworld. This is not an easy technique to master and indeed for some people it will prove impossible as each Witch has different talents, however, it is important to try. Don't be discouraged when it takes time to get the basics of these techniques down and if you do not initially get any response or have any success. More so than with other methods, journey work requires a great deal of practice.

The first challenge is learning to know when your spirit is actually traveling out and when you are experiencing your own imagination. A good rule of thumb is to look at whether what happens or what is said is what you expected or if it is a surprise; generally, if everything that happens is exactly as you'd expect then that is a sign that you are imagining things, whereas, if things are unexpected or not what you would want that can indicate a genuine experience. In the same way, you should try to influence the experience as it is occurring – if you can affect things by changing your surroundings, or influencing the words or actions of beings around you, then you are likely imagining the situation, when on a genuine spiritual journey, you will find the beings you meet are autonomous and beyond your influence.

Secondly, you need to know how to protect yourself and how to get out quickly in emergencies. Spiritual journey work is not 100 percent safe and it is possible to be psychically injured in a journey if you are not careful. Even if you are careful, you may be hurt, and it is good to study methods of psychic healing so that you can take off anything that might come up. Allies are one aspect of protection, but you can also work on your visualization and manifestation skills to create things in the Otherworld to use to defend yourself. It's important to remember not to be needlessly threatening to other beings, but also that not every-thing you meet will be friendly and that some of the fairies you meet may try to harm you. Try never to offer insult to anything, even if it is threatening you, but also be willing to stand up for yourself. Protective chants that work in our world also work in Faery, so it is good to memorize a few. Also, practice quickly returning to normal consciousness when you need to.

The first basic journey to go on is the one to find your guide. This may take more than one attempt, so don't get discouraged. Once you find a fairy being that seems friendly towards you and willing to be helpful to you, you can ask it if it is willing to guide you when you are in Faery. Be very precise in your wording and make sure you are clear in what you would like the fairy to do for you. This is a sample of what a Fairy Guide journey might look like, this can also be used as a guided meditation.

Fairy Guide Journey

Sit or rest comfortably in a quiet place where you won't be disturbed. Close your eyes and breathe deeply, sending down energetic roots into the earth. See these roots anchoring you in the world as you pull up energy. When you feel fully centered, send your spirit outwards into the mist of Faery.

Feel the mist surrounding you as you move from this world into the Otherworld. You feel solid earth beneath your feet and find yourself standing in a clearing in a thick wood. Trees grow densely all around you and you can hear birdsong and the rustle of animals in the underbrush. Look around and familiarize yourself with this place; in the center of the clearing is a stone with a symbol carved on it. This place is your gateway to and from the Otherworld and it is where you will enter and exit as you learn to travel there.

Find a place to sit in the clearing and wait to see if any fairies choose to join you. Be open to whatever shape or form the fairy may take; it could appear as a human-seeming being or as an animal, or even as a light or plant. If you are joined by anything, greet it politely and see how it reacts to you. Is it silent? Is it hostile? Does it greet you in return? Try talking with it and see what it has to say.

If the conversation goes well you might decide to ask the fairy if it is willing to be your friend. If it seems interested, ask it if it is willing to help keep you safe and guide you when you are in Faery. Do not be offended if it says no, as this represents a significant commitment on the fairy's part, but if it agrees, ask it what it would like in return. Keep in mind that if what it wants is too much or too difficult for you to do, you can always politely decline – remember never to say 'thank you' though! If its terms are agreeable, then tell the fairy that you are willing to give it what it wants in exchange for it acting as your guide and helping to protect you; if it agrees, then you have a fairy guide.

Once the conversation is finished and the fairy has left, see the mist rising again and feel the clearing in the wood disappearing as the mist pulls you back. Follow the ties back to your body and feel your spirit settling back down into its place. Draw energy up from the earth and then slowly pull up the energetic roots you sent down at the beginning. Breathe deeply, stretch and get up slowly.

This is also a good journey to do on the dark moon and whenever you want to connect to your fairy allies.

Through The Veil – A Life Saved

I do not always make good choices. Despite having been an EMT, when it comes to myself, I tend to dismiss or minimize health problems. One night I had a severe allergic reaction, and instead of doing what I should and calling an ambulance, I did exactly the wrong thing and decided to go to bed. I didn't want to bother anybody, it was late, and I felt that I'd be inconveniencing people. So I was lying in bed with my tongue starting to swell trying to ignore how serious this all was when suddenly my husband leaped out of bed yelling. He swore that a huge moth had just flown into his face although he could find no sign of it, or anything else, anywhere. I felt a wave of calm go over me and heard a voice say, 'Now, be sensible, get up, and get help.' So I did, an ambulance was called, and thanks to the paramedic, I lived to see another day.

To this day I have no doubt that it was a fairy that saved me.

Chapter 9

Magic

In Fairy Witchcraft, magic is a cornerstone to practice and is essential to learn and to actively do. Magic is intrinsic in every aspect of my life. I say a blessing charm over every meal I cook, whisper protective prayers over my children before they leave the house, give my family medicine along with healing spells when they are sick. There are also the greater magics when needed – such as the fith fath and the Druid mist – but it's these little daily magics that are part of my life, morning and night. If my life is a song that I am singing as I go, then magic is the constant tide of breathing that underlies each verse and chorus. And I wouldn't want it any other way.

An entire book could be written on Fairy Witchcraft magic alone, but I wanted to include examples of different types of charms and spells commonly used to at least give the reader an idea of the general style of magic.

The *Carmina Gadelica* has a series of charms which all deal with the evil eye, that is the curse laid upon a person by another who wishes them ill or looks upon them with envy. This one is my personal favorite and I have modified it slightly to be more pagan; I love the imagery it presents and find it reminiscent of the Song of Amergin. Anyone who has read the works of the Witch Sibyl Leek may recognize the middle portion of the charm, the 'power over' section, as she made use of this portion in an unhexing spell in one of her books, clearly drawing on the *Gadelica* as a source. That same section has also appeared in a young adult novel by L. J. Smith called *The Power*; all of which could be seen as a testament to the power and flexibility of the *Carmina Gadelica* charms, as well as their intrinsic value.

Exorcism of the Evil Eye 141

I trample upon the evil eye,
As the duck tramples upon the lake,
As the swan tramples upon the water,
As the horse tramples upon the plain,
As the cow tramples upon the grass,
As the host tramples the sky,
As the host tramples the air.
Power of wind I have over it,
Power of wrath I have over it,
Power of fire I have over it,
Power of thunder I have over it,
Power of lightning I have over it,
Power of storms I have over it,
Power of moon I have over it,
Power of sun I have over it,
Power of stars I have over it,
Power of earth I have over it,
Power of sky and of the worlds I have over it,
Power of the sky and of the worlds I have over it.
A portion of it upon the grey stones,
A portion of it upon the steep hills,
A portion of it upon the fast falls,
A portion of it upon the fair meadows,
And a portion upon the great salt sea,
She herself is the best instrument to carry it,
The great salt sea,
is the best instrument to carry it.
In the names of the Three of Life,
In the names of the Gods of Skill,
In the names of all the Ancient Ones,
And of the Powers together.
Excerpt from *By Land, Sea, and Sky* by the author

To Call Rain

Grind ferns in your mortar and pestle and then add to fresh water in a small cauldron or bowl and pour out onto the earth.

To Heal a Joint Pain

Take your fairy stone and rub it on the joint from the top down towards the earth. Chant:

Wear away, wear away
Here you shall not stay
I cast you far away
Away, away, away.

To Reduce Tumors or Swelling

The charm should be chanted while holding your hands over the afflicted area, or a picture of the person. I highly recommend doing this charm on a set regular basis, for example three times a day for a series of nine or 27 days. In order for the charm to be effective it must be done often and consistently. Chant:

Nine waves upon the ocean
The nine become eight,
The eight become seven,
The seven become six,
The six become five,
The five become four,
The four become three,
The three become two,
The two become one,
One becomes none;
Out from the marrow into the blood,
Out from the blood into the flesh,
Out from the flesh into the skin,
Out from the skin into the hair,

Out from the hair to the healing earth

Four Thieves Vinegar

Four Thieves Vinegar is an herbal vinegar mixture that has been used, so the story goes, since the time of the Black Death. According to the myth, during the time of the plague four thieves were caught robbing the dead and dying; in exchange for their lives they revealed a secret blend of herbs and vinegar that they were using to keep from getting sick – hence the name Four Thieves Vinegar.

Most recipes for Four Thieves are edible and make a yummy salad dressing, or can be used in any other way that vinegar could be. Some people swear by Four Thieves Vinegar as a health tonic and include it in their diet every day, and others believe that it will prevent contagious diseases. It is generally viewed as an immunity booster. As with anything else, if you intend to use it in food be sure you know what's in it (if you are buying it) and store it properly. If you make it yourself, be sure to use herbs that are edible and that are safe for you personally to use with your own medical history – it is always a good idea to consult an herbalist or doctor before using any herbs medicinally, to be certain it will be safe for you to do so.

In magic, it is used for protection and banishing; it is good for getting people to leave, unhexing, uncrossing, protecting your aura, and protection against magical attack. I also use it in healing work. There are many different ways to use Four Thieves Vinegar, limited really only by your own imagination. It can be added to cleansing baths to clear out negative energy, break another person's negative magic being sent at you, and to strengthen your own protections for a time.

You can use it to anoint candles for any purpose related to Four Thieves Vinegar's reputed effects. A little bit could be dabbed on the forehead for cleansing or protection as well. To banish others, it can be added to banishing spells or dripped out on the person's footsteps; it can also be used as an ink (symbolically but effectively) or added to a Witch's' bottle for protection. If adding to a Witch's bottle, I would recommend an alternate version of Four Thieves used in Hoodoo, made with different types of peppers and garlic.

There are many different recipes for Four Thieves vinegar, which can be made with any type of vinegar and with any combination of the following herbs: rosemary, lavender, garlic, lemon balm, sage, hyssop, peppermint, wormwood, juniper, eucalyptus, cinnamon, clove, pepper, or marjoram. To make Four Thieves Vinegar, a selection of herbs – generally three to seven – are placed in the vinegar, and the bottle is then stored in a cool, dark location. Each day for six weeks the bottle should be gentle shaken, and then after six weeks the vinegar can be transferred to another container for use. There are, naturally, many other ways to make it as well.

You can, of course, buy it but I prefer to make my own and I have two different types I use. One I make with white vinegar and the other with cider vinegar; each I think has slightly different properties. I generally add herbs I have grown myself, have found wild, or which have been given to me by the person who grew them. I tend to favor using sage, rosemary, lavender, mullein, and wormwood, personally, but each batch tends to involve a little variety.

Websites for Further Reading on Four Thieves Vinegar
http://www.luckymojo.com/spells/recipes.html
http://prettysmartnaturalideas.wordpress.com/2007/12/11/four-
    thieves-vinegar-oil-recipes/
http://www.advance-health.com/fourthievesvinegar.html
http://nourishedkitchen.com/four-thieves-vinegar-recipe/
http://www.livestrong.com/article/287639-the-health-benefits-of-
    four-thieves-vinegar/

Witch Bottles

One of my favorite traditional methods of protection in Witchcraft is a Witch's bottle. It's fairly simple to make, yet easily added to or adapted, and once made is set in place and then requires no maintenance. It's effective, yet subtle. And it's something that anyone can do, no matter what the skill or experience level.

A Witch's bottle is a type of folk charm that is designed to attract and trap any negative energy or malicious magic sent your way, so that it is prevented from causing you any harm. Many modern sites talk about using Witch bottles for different purposes, along the lines of a charm.

This may work well for others, but I stick to the traditional use – if I want a charm for money or love I'll just make one for that instead of using a Witch bottle. Witch bottles were a common folk charm used throughout the 16th and 17th centuries to protect people from negative magic; more than 200 Witch bottles have been found buried throughout Europe, but most are broken by the time they are uncovered (Viegas, 2009).

An example of an American Witch bottle was found in Pennsylvania that dates to the 18th century, and the practice was common enough in America that preachers spoke out against its use, although it was also recommended by other contemporaries, including Cotton Mathers, as a good protection against Witches (Becker, 2009). During a period when many people feared Witchcraft, the Witch bottle offered a sense of security and protection and allowed people to proactively defend themselves when they felt they may be the victim of a curse. In modern practice a Witch's bottle is still an excellent tool to use to protect yourself from any possible negative magic, rather like a magical electric fence.

Examination of a Witch bottle found in Greenwich that dates to the 17th century showed the contents to be similar to those that are still used today: urine, sulfur, nail clippings, nails, and pins

(Viegas, 2009). Many examples of Witch bottles also include a felt, cloth, or leather heart pierced by a pin as well, although the exact purpose of this is unknown (Becker, 2009; Viegas, 2009). It was believed that the pins and nails would turn the magic back on to the caster, while the urine and nail clippings would draw the magic intended for the person to the bottle instead; often the ingredients would be boiled together first (Becker, 2009). Historical examples are found buried, often top down, in front of a house with the intent of protecting the home or a specific inhabitant from malicious magic (Becker, 2009). The bottles used were the type commonly seen in those areas for drinking and could be stoneware, ceramic, or glass, with a specific type called a 'Bellermine' often used. The Bellermine was named after a Catholic cardinal whose face appeared stamped on the bottles.

In modern practice, the bottles would be made and used in much the same way as they were historically. To make one you need a glass or ceramic bottle that can be corked or sealed at the top. For a basic bottle add your own urine and nail clippings, some hair, sulfur, nails and pins; if you want you can include the felt heart as well. The bottle can be modified with other materials such as herbs – agrimony or blessed thistle work well for anticurse magic, or for something stronger, mandrake or belladonna could be used, for example, broken glass, mirrors, or peppers. Add the urine first – on a practical note I recommend using a cup to collect it and then pouring it into the bottle – then add the other items. Traditionally, the mixture would be boiled before being added to the bottle. Once the bottle is full seal the top, and if you'd like to, say something to charge the bottle with its purpose.

When complete, bury the bottle near the front of your home where it won't be found or disturbed; although some people who live in an apartment or otherwise have no land to bury it in might choose to keep it hidden under a sink or bury it in a potted plant inside the home. If you move do not disturb the old bottle (although if it is under your sink don't leave it there!), rather make a new bottle for your new home.

Through The Veil – Moonlight Magic

In May 2012 we had what was widely touted as a 'super moon', an unusually large and bright full moon. The night of the super moon, after my family went to sleep, I went out into the night beneath the moonlight. I brought nothing with me, but the air itself was charged with magic. I opened myself to it and let the energy show me the way to go. A thick silence fell over the neighborhood, but underneath it a delicate sound of bells could be heard. Beneath the shadows of the oaks I danced around the hawthorn tree in my yard. I raised a whirlwind of energy as I danced and I started to sing out to the night. I sang to the liminal Gods. I sang to the fairies. I sang to the moon and the night. I blessed my home and my family and poured out the energy I raised as an offering to the Powers I had called. When I was done, I stood beneath the night sky and simply breathed.

I had gone out just after 11pm. I thought perhaps half an hour or 45 minutes had gone by when I finally went back in, but glancing at a clock showed the truth – three hours had passed.

Conclusion

Everything that you have read here is the heart of my own belief and practice of Witchcraft. The path of Fairy Witchcraft is neither easy nor safe, but it can be very rewarding. It is a path of mystery and enchantment, ultimately solitary and yet never alone.

When I first sat down to write this book I wasn't sure if it was even a good idea to do so; I have never spoken about these things in any depth to anyone, nor taught anyone my practices except for my own children. And the first thing I tell people when I teach classes about fairies is that they should be approached with extreme caution and dealt with very carefully. To encourage people to do the opposite of that, to not only make the usual Fairy Faith offerings to appease the fairies but also to reach out to them as allies – to encourage risk and danger – is not something I would usually do. But the old ways are slowly being lost as fewer and fewer practice them and the new ways that people relate to fairies with are very different from the old Fairy Faith. My ways may not be exactly like the old cunningfolk and fairy doctors, but for those seeking to follow the old Fairy Faith and practice neo-pagan Witchcraft this system does work. Perhaps it is exactly what someone reading this now has been seeking.

More than all of this, though, I believe that the Good Neighbors want the old beliefs to be preserved and the old ways to continue on. There was a time, not so long ago, when in some places everyone believed in fairies as beautiful and fearsome beings that deserved respect, but that isn't so anymore. I hope that by writing this those ways can be preserved and continued on, in some small way.

While writing this book I had many experiences which encouraged me to keep writing and to be totally honest. The day I finished I found a four leaf clover, only the second one I have ever found in my life. I believe I have said what they wanted me to say.

Appendix A

Self-Dedication Ritual

If you are certain that Fairy Witchcraft is the path for you then you can perform a ritual to dedicate yourself to following it and to following the liminal Gods. There is no need for a ritual to dedicate to honoring the fairies, as that is less about words than it is about actions; however, the charm pouch you will make for this dedication ritual does also symbolize your honoring of those spirits.

Make a small pouch out of green silk or cloth that you can wear around your neck. In the pouch place some earth from your home, nine herbs for luck, blessing, protection, health, power, wisdom, magic and at least one of the nine should be a fairy plant. Add tokens from three animals whose qualities you want to draw to yourself. Add three drops of your own blood on a small piece of cloth and a lock of hair. Tie the pouch closed and place it on your altar.

Cast a circle to open a portal to the Otherworld and call in your ancestors, the goodly-inclined fairies, and all of the liminal Gods. Light a white candle and say:

Gods of the Otherworld,
Everlasting joy
Is in my soul
With good intent.
And for every gift of peace
You bestow on me.
My thoughts, my words,
My deeds, my desires
I dedicate to You.
I make offerings to You,

As I ask for Your protection,
And Your guidance,
Shield me tonight,
And walk with me each day.

Make an offering of oats, honey, and milk to each of the Powers you have invoked. Then pick up the pouch and say:

I am a Witch
I respect the fairy folk
I honor my ancestors,
I worship the Old Gods
From this day forth
I walk the path
Of Fairy Witchcraft
Joyous and solemn
Foolish and wise
Wild and gentle
I am a Witch.

Put the pouch on. Close the circle. It is done. You should wear the pouch every day, but especially whenever you are doing any magic.

Appendix B

Resources

Fiction
Hounds of the Morrigan by Pat O'Shea
The SERRAted Edge series and the Bedlam's Bard series by Mercedes Lackey

Websites
Ashliman, D., (2009) Fairy Gifts. Retrieved May 24, 2012 from http://www.pitt.edu/~dash/type0503.html
Lawless, S., (2009) Fairy Faiths. Retrieved April 8, 2012 from http://Witchofforestgrove.com/2009/09/15/fairy-traditions/
Whittier, J., (2008) Charms and Fairy Faith. Retrieved April 8, 2012 from http://www.readbookonline.net/readOnLine/8364/
Yeats, W. B, (1888) Fairy and Folk Tales of the Irish Peasantry. Retrieved May 24, 2012 from http://www.sacred-texts.com/neu/yeats/fip/index.htm

Movies
The Secret of Roan Inish, (1995) Sony Pictures
Into the West (2011) Echo Bridge Home Entertainment
The Secret of Kells, (2010) New Video Group
Fairy Faith, (2001) Wellspring Media
The Secret World of Arietty, (2012) Buena Vista
The Spiderwick Chronicles, (2008) Paramount
Labyrinth, (1986) Sony Pictures
Pan's Labyrinth, (2007) New Line Home Video
The Lord of The Rings, (2002) New Line
The Hobbit, (2012) New Line
Hellboy II: The Golden Army, (2008) Universal Studios

Bibliography

Becker, M., (2009) An American Witch Bottle. Retrieved from http://www.archaeology.org/online/features/halloween/Witch _bottle.html

Bord, J., (1997) Fairies: Real Encounters with Little People

Campbell, J., (2005) The Gaelic Otherworld

Carmichael, A., (1900) Carmina Gadelica

Cunningham, S., (1985) Cunningham's Encyclopedia of Magical Herbs

Daimler, M. (2010) By Land, Sea, and Sky

Daimler, M. (2012) A Child's Eye View of the Fairy Faith

Danaher (1972) The Year in Ireland

Danaher (1964) Irish Customs and Beliefs

DeVries, L., (2010). Red Clover., http://medicinalherbinfo.org/ herbs/RedClover.html

Ellis Davidson, H., (1988) Myths and Symbols in Pagan Europe

Estyn Evans, E., (1957) Irish Folk Ways

Evans-Wentz, W. Y., (1911) The Fairy Faith in Celtic Countries

Evert Hopman, E., (2011) Scottish Herbs and Fairy Lore

Foster, S., and Duke, J., (2000) A Field Guide to Medicinal Plants and Herbs: of Eastern and Central North America

Fraser Black, G., (1894) Scottish Charms and Amulets

Freeman, P., (2008) War, Women, and Druids

Froud, B., and Lee, A., (2002) Faeries

Froud, B., (1998) Good Faeries, Bad Faeries

Gray, E., (1983) Cath Maige Tuired

Green, M., (1997) The World of the Druids

Gregory, L., (1988) A Treasury of Irish Myth, Legend & Folklore

Grieve, M., (1971) A Modern Herbal

Gundarsson, K., (2007) Elves, Wights and Trolls

Kirk, R., (2006) The Secret Commonwealth of Elves, Fauns and Fairies

Lecouteux, C., (1999) Phantom Armies of the Night: The Wild Hunt and the Ghostly Processions of the Undead

Lenihan and Green, (2004) Meeting the Other Crowd

MacGillivray, Deborah, (2000) The Cait Sidhe. Retrieved from http://deborahmacgillivray.co.uk/scotlore_caitsidhe.htm

Matthews, C., and J., (2005) The Elemental Encyclopedia of Magical Creatures

Matthews, J., (1997) The Druid Source Book

MacAlister, R., (1941) Lebor Gabala Erenn

McNeill, F., (1956) The Silver Bough, volume 1

McNeill, F., (1959) The Silver Bough, volume 2

McNeill, F., (1961) The Silver Bough, volume 3

Miller, J., (2004) Magic and Witchcraft in Scotland

O hOgain, D., (1995) Irish Superstitions

O Suilleabhain, S., (1967). Nosanna agus Piseoga na nGael

Old Farmer's Almanac (2012) http://www.almanac.com/calendar/date/2012-08-17

Plant Life (2012) White Clover, http://montana.plant-life.org/species/trifol_repe.htm

Ross, A., (1970) Pagan Celts

Viegas, S., (2009). 17th Century Urine-filled Witch Bottle Found. Retrieved from http://www.msnbc.msn.com/id/31107319/ns/technology_and_science-science/t/th-century-urine-filled-Witch-bottle-found/

Viking Answer Lady (n.d.) Sacred Space in Viking Law and Religion. Retrieved from http://www.vikinganswerlady.com/sacspace.shtml

Walsh, B., (2002) The Secret Commonwealth and the Fairy Belief Complex

White, C., (2005) A History of Irish Fairies

Wilby, E., (2005) Cunning Folk and Familiar Spirits

Wilde, L. (1991) Irish Cures, Mystic Charms & Superstition

Yeats, W. B., (1962) The Celtic Twilight

Yeats, W. B., (1998) Fairy and Folktales of Ireland

Yeats, W. B., (1888) Fairy and Folk Tales of the Irish Peasantry. Retrieved from http://www.sacred-texts.com/neu/yeats/fip/

MOON

BOOKS

Moon Books invites you to begin or deepen your encounter with Paganism, in all its rich, creative, flourishing forms.